# 200 VEG

HAMLYN **ALL COLOUR COOKBOOK**

# 200

## VEGGIE FEASTS

**LOUISE PICKFORD**

An Hachette UK Company
www.hachette.co.uk

First published in Great Britain in 2008 by Hamlyn,
a division of Octopus Publishing Group Ltd,
Carmelite House, 50 Victoria Embankment,
London EC4Y 0DZ
www.octopusbooks.co.uk

This edition published in 2016

ISBN 978-0-600-63337-2

A CIP catalogue record for this book is available
from the British Library

Printed and bound in China

10 9 8 7 6 5 4 3 2 1

Standard level spoon measurement are used in all recipes.
1 tablespoon = one 15 ml spoon
1 teaspoon = one 5 ml spoon

Both imperial and metric measures have been given in all
recipes. Use one set of measurements only and not a
mixture of both.

Eggs should be medium unless otherwise stated. The
Department of Health advises that eggs should not be
consumed raw. This book contains dishes made with raw or
lightly cooked eggs. It is prudent for more vulnerable people
such as pregnant and nursing mothers, invalids, the elderly,
babies and young children to avoid uncooked or lightly
cooked dishes made with eggs. Once prepared these dishes
should be kept refrigerated and used promptly.

Ovens should be preheated to the specific temperature –
if using a fan-assisted oven, follow the manufacturer's
instructions for adjusting the time and the temperature.

This book includes dishes made with nuts and nut
derivatives. It is advisable for customers with known allergic
reactions to nuts and nut derivatives and those who may
be potentially vulnerable to these allergies, such as pregnant
and nursing mothers, invalids, the elderly, babies and
children, to avoid dishes made with nuts and nut oils. It is
also prudent to check the labels of pre-prepared ingredients
for the possible inclusion of nut derivatives.

Vegetarians should look for the 'V' symbol on a cheese to
ensure it is made with vegetarian rennet.

# contents

introduction      6

breakfast & brunch      14

starters & snacks      40

main meals      72

soups & stews      108

salads & sides      138

breads & baking      172

desserts      198

index      236

acknowledgements      240

# introduction

# introduction

Today, choosing to eat a vegetarian diet is far easier than it ever was, with such high-quality and varied produce to choose from in our supermarkets and food stores. Whether you are a vegetarian yourself, cooking for a vegetarian or just looking for some inspirational meat-free recipes to enjoy from time to time, this book is packed with exciting and innovative ideas for everyday meals. Each recipe is expertly photographed so that you can see exactly what you will be cooking, and every one offers a creative variation, giving a total of 200 recipes in one handy package!

## time factor
Because time is so precious to us in our modern hectic world, getting a meal on the

table as speedily as possible is paramount, and this book has been specifically designed with that in mind, offering a wide range of versatile quick-and-easy dishes. Since many of these delicious recipes can be prepared and cooked in 30 minutes or less, any lingering concern you may have that vegetarian food is more involved and time-consuming to cook than meat-based food, will soon be consigned to myth.

To help us cook more efficiently, we need to shop well, so that everything we require is on hand or can be bought on the way home from work. If you forward plan your week, shopping for staples and non-perishables in one go, you can then simply pick up fresh ingredients as and when you need them. A well-stocked storecupboard is invaluable, so make sure you always have the basics at your fingertips, such as extra virgin olive oil, balsamic vinegar, sea salt, canned tomatoes and beans, dried lentils, pasta, rice and flour.

## healthy choices
Although a vegetarian diet doesn't guarantee better health, any risk associated with eating red meat is obviously eliminated. Unless you are vegan, you will most likely be consuming other animal products, including eggs, cheese, butter, cream and milk, but it is important to

processed foods. Always purchase fruit, vegetables and herbs in the best, freshest condition possible to gain the maximum nutritional benefits. There is a far greater choice now when it comes to buying organic, but it remains the more expensive option. It is always worthwhile purchasing organic free-range eggs, but beyond that, you can choose which organic produce to buy according to your budget and what looks best on the day.

And remember that the only sure-fire way of knowing exactly what we are eating is to make our meals ourselves. So start cooking now and enjoy some really fabulous vegetarian food.

avoid the common trap of over-compensating for the lack of meat by consuming, in particular, large quantities of cheese, which is high in saturated fats that can lead to heart disease. A balanced diet is vital in providing our bodies with the right amount of proteins, carbohydrates, essential fats, vitamins and minerals to maintain good health. We can do this by eating plenty of fresh fruit and vegetables (the recommended daily intake is five servings per day), as well as pulses, grains and soya products combined with sensible amounts of eggs, milk and cheese.

To get the most from our food, we need to buy good-quality fresh ingredients and avoid

## storing fresh ingredients

Once you have bought the best quality ingredients it is important to use them as soon as possible, or to store them so that they maintain as much freshness as possible.

Most fruits and vegetables should be kept in the refrigerator, but those that don't chill – such as potatoes, onions, garlic, apples and other high-starch foods – should be kept in a cool dark place, preferably in paper bags.

Unless you have bought herbs in pots, I find the best method for keeping them perky is to place them in a large zip-lock bag with a sprinkle of cold water. Seal the bag and store in the refrigerator.

## recipes for every occasion

The book is divided into seven chapters, designed to make choosing the type of dish you want to cook ultra easy. If you are looking for a snack or a main meal, a side salad and a dessert, each recipe can be found in its respective chapter. Planning a dinner party? You can quickly put a menu together by searching through the appropriate chapters to find exactly what you want. And with a useful variation for each recipe, you have double the choice.

Vegetarian options may seem limited for **breakfast & brunch**, but here you will find lots of delicious ideas to nourish and satisfy any discerning diner. Try the wickedly rich and indulgent Rocket & Goats' Cheese Omelette (see page 18) or feed family and friends in laid-back style with the washing-up

friendly All-In-One Veggie Breakfast (see page 22).

Many of the great-tasting dishes in **starters & snacks** will suit either role, making them particularly versatile. There are several that can be ready to eat in less than 20 minutes, such as the rather exotic-sounding Haloumi with Pomegranate Salsa (see page 42) or the Bean, Lemon & Rosemary Hummus (see page 68) – a delicious bean pâté.

What you will find surprisingly refreshing about the **main meals** chapter is that many of the recipes are not stereotypically vegetarian. Rather, they are dishes that meat-eaters and non-meat-eaters alike will yearn for and eat regularly, such as the Creamy Pea & Mint Risotto with Brie (see page 80), Spinach & Ricotta Cannelloni (see page 100) or Broad Bean & Lemon Spaghetti (see page 82).

The **soups & stews** chapter features quick-and-easy soup recipes suitable for everyday family meals, as well as others that would make the perfect starter to any dinner party, such as the indulgent Mushroom Soup with Truffle Butter (see page 112). A few of the dishes are more substantial stews, ideal for a chilly winter's night – for example, the wonderfully hearty Goulash with Chive Dumplings (see page 130).

In **salads & sides** you will find some enduring classics, but most dishes offer a

things in life. Why not try the simple but totally divine Rich Chocolate Mousse (see page 200), so easy to make that you won't believe it. Or for a really special occasion, perhaps when friends are over for dinner, make the Tiramisù Cheesecake (see page 212) – those familiar flavours never tasted so good.

## ingredients guide

The following are some useful, practical notes on some of the ingredients featured in the recipes, including the more unusual items.

### eggs

Always buy free-range, preferably organic eggs. If you keep your eggs in the refrigerator, always remove them and leave at room temperature for 1 hour before use.

modern twist on the more traditional recipe, such as Roast Vegetables & Parsley Pesto (see page 160) or the Baked Sweet Potatoes (see page 166), filled with soured cream and chives. Some of the dishes make great accompaniments to main meals, while others could provide a tasty light lunch.

There is something wonderfully comforting about the thought of home baking and you will find a whole variety of enticing recipes in **breads & baking**. The heavenly smell of freshly baked bread is hard to beat and what better way to ensure a delicious supper than to bake a savoury tart. You will be amazed at just how easy it is to make your own pizzas – the Roasted Squash & Sage Pizza (see page 192) is a revelation!

Last, but never least, is a chapter on **desserts**, because we all need to indulge from time to time in some of the sweeter

### buttermilk

This is the liquid that remains after cream is churned into butter. Similar to milk but with less fat and a slightly sour taste, it is a great alternative to both milk and yogurt, and can be found in the chill cabinet in supermarkets and health-food stores.

### haloumi cheese

A hard, salty sheep's milk cheese from Cyprus, haloumi is always eaten cooked and should be consumed as soon as it melts, as it can become rather chewy when it cools.

### fontina cheese

This is a mild Italian cows' milk cheese that melts really well. You can also substitute mozzarella cheese, which has a milder flavour. Fontina is available from some of

the larger supermarkets, Italian delis and specialist food stores.

### taleggio cheese

This soft Italian cows' milk cheese is similar to Brie, which could be used instead. It is available from cheese shops, Italian delis and some larger supermarkets.

### arborio rice

A medium-grain rice grown in Italy, arborio is traditionally used to make risotto, as its high starch content adds a creamy consistency to the finished dish. It is widely available.

### polenta

An Italian maize-like porridge, polenta can be served soft or left to set, cut into squares and chargrilled. The grain itself is also known as cornmeal, which you can use instead. Instant polenta is used in the recipes in this book.

### ramen noodles

These are traditional Japanese dried noodles available from Asian food stores. There are several types of dried noodles used in Japanese soups, and you can choose any of these for the recipes in this book.

### savoiardi biscuits

These thin, finger-shaped biscuits topped with sugar are traditionally used to make tiramisù. They are widely available.

### herbs

Always use fresh herbs whenever possible. If you have to use dried herbs, use half the amount specified in the ingredients list. Why not buy some potted herbs and keep on the windowsill for a cheaper option?

### kaffir lime leaves

These are the fragrant leaves of the Kaffir lime tree. They are used extensively in Thai cooking and are available fresh from most good greengrocers, Asian food stores and some supermarkets. You can freeze fresh leaves and use them straight from the freezer.

### vegetable stock

Always use a good-quality vegetable stock. Often bouillon powders are superior to stock cubes, but it is best to try out several varieties to find the one you like best.

### vincotto

This is an Italian condiment made from dried grape must that is boiled to a thick syrup and aged in oak barrels. It is similar to aged balsamic vinegar. It is available from some Italian delis, specialist food stores and internet suppliers.

### marsala

This is a fortified wine from Sicily with a deep colour and wonderful spicy aroma. It is the traditional flavouring in tiramisù and also makes a delicious aperitif.

### tahini paste

Made from ground sesame seeds, this paste is used extensively in North African cooking and is widely available from health-food stores.

### mirin

This is a spirit-based, sweet liquid used in Japanese cooking, and is available from larger supermarkets, Asian food stores and health-food stores.

### wakame seaweed

This dried seaweed is used in Japanese cooking, and adds a deep flavour to stocks and soups. It is available from health-food stores.

# breakfast &
# brunch

# parmesan eggy bread

Serves **6**
Preparation time **10 minutes**
Cooking time **8–14 minutes**

**6 plum tomatoes**
4 tablespoons ready-made
   **olive tapenade**
**extra virgin olive oil**, for
   drizzling
150 ml (¼ pint) **milk**
**3 eggs**
3 tablespoons freshly grated
   **Parmesan cheese**
50 g (2 oz) **butter**
6 slices of **white bread**
handful of **baby spinach
   leaves**
a few **basil leaves**, to serve
**salt and black pepper**

**Cut** the tomatoes in half and scoop out the seeds. Arrange cut-side up in a baking dish. Spoon a little of the tapenade on to each tomato and drizzle over some oil. Cook under a preheated hot grill for 2–3 minutes until soft and golden. Keep warm.

**Beat** the milk, eggs, Parmesan and a little salt and pepper together in a bowl. Pour into a shallow dish. Melt half the butter in a large frying pan. Dip 3 bread slices into the egg mixture, add to the pan and fry over a medium heat for 3–4 minutes, turning once, until golden on both sides. Remove and keep warm in a moderate oven. Repeat with the remaining bread slices and egg mixture.

**Serve** the eggy bread topped with the grilled tomatoes, baby spinach leaves and a few basil leaves.

**For sweet eggy bread**, dip 4 slices of brioche into a mixture of 2 beaten eggs, 25 g (1 oz) caster sugar and ½ teaspoon ground cinnamon. Melt 25 g (1 oz) butter in a frying pan, add half the bread slices and fry for 2–3 minutes on each side until golden. Repeat with the remaining brioche slices and egg mixture. Serve the bread dusted with icing sugar, topped with fresh berries and a dollop of whipped cream.

# rocket & goats' cheese omelette

Serves **4**
Preparation time **5 minutes**
Cooking time **12 minutes**

12 **eggs**
4 tablespoons **milk**
4 tablespoons chopped
  **mixed herbs**, such as
  chervil, chives, marjoram,
  parsley and tarragon
50 g (2 oz) **butter**
125 g (4 oz) **soft goats'
  cheese**, diced
small handful of **baby rocket
  leaves**
**salt and black pepper**

**Beat** the eggs, milk, herbs and salt and pepper together in a large bowl. Melt a quarter of the butter in an omelette pan. As soon as it stops foaming, swirl in a quarter of the egg mixture and cook over a medium heat, forking over the omelette so that it cooks evenly.

**As** soon as it is set on the underside, but still a little runny in the centre, scatter a quarter of the cheese and a quarter of the rocket leaves over one half of the omelette. Carefully slide the omelette on to a warmed serving plate, folding it in half as you go. For the best results, serve immediately, then repeat to make 3 more omelettes and serve each individually. Alternatively, keep warm in a moderate oven and serve altogether.

**For cheese & tomato omelette**, follow the recipe above to the end of the first stage. Then top each omelette with 15 g (½ oz) grated Cheddar cheese and 25 g (1 oz) halved cherry tomatoes. Carefully tip the omelette out on to a warmed plate, folding in half as you go. Repeat to make 3 more omelettes.

# boiled egg with mustard soldiers

Serves **4**
Preparation time **5 minutes**
Cooking time **5 minutes**

2 teaspoons **wholegrain
    mustard**, or to taste
50 g (2 oz) **unsalted butter**,
    softened
4 large **eggs**
4 thick slices of **white bread**
**black pepper**
**mustard and cress**, to serve

**Beat** the mustard, butter and pepper together in a small bowl.

**Cook** the eggs in a saucepan of boiling water for 4–5 minutes until softly set. Meanwhile, toast the bread, then butter one side with the mustard butter and cut into fingers.

**Serve** the eggs with the mustard soldiers and some mustard and cress.

**For boiled egg with asparagus**, replace the toasted soldiers with freshly steamed asparagus spears. Trim 2 bunches of asparagus spears and peel the stems. Steam or boil for 2 minutes until tender and serve with the boiled egg to dip.

# all-in-one veggie breakfast

Serves **4**
Preparation time **10 minutes**
Cooking time **35 minutes**

500 g (1 lb) **cooked
    potatoes**, cubed
4 tablespoons **olive oil**
a few **thyme** sprigs
250 g (8 oz) **button
    mushrooms**, trimmed
12 **cherry tomatoes**
4 **eggs**
**salt and black pepper**
2 tablespoons chopped
    **parsley**, to garnish
**buttered toast**, to serve
    (optional)

**Spread** the potato cubes out in a roasting tin. Drizzle over half the oil, scatter over the thyme sprigs and season with salt and pepper. Bake in a preheated oven, 220°C (425°F), Gas Mark 7, for 10 minutes.

**Stir** the potato cubes well, then add the mushrooms and bake for 10 minutes. Add the tomatoes and bake for a further 10 minutes.

**Make** four hollows in between the vegetables and carefully break an egg into each hollow. Bake for 3–4 minutes until the eggs are set. Garnish the vegetable mixture with the parsley and serve straight from the tin, with buttered toast.

**For all-in-one veggie supper**, without the eggs, use 750 g (1½ lb) potatoes and 400 g (13 oz) mushrooms. Follow the recipe as above, sprinkling 125 g (4 oz) Cheddar cheese over the vegetables for the final 10 minutes of cooking.

# cheese, tomato & basil muffins

Makes **8**
Preparation time **10 minutes**
Cooking time **20–25 minutes**

**spray oil**, for oiling
150 g (5 oz) **self-raising flour**
½ teaspoon **salt**
100 g (3½ oz) **fine cornmeal**
65 g (2½ oz) **Cheddar cheese**, grated
50 g (2 oz) drained **sun-dried tomatoes** in oil, chopped
2 tablespoons chopped **basil**
1 **egg**, lightly beaten
300 ml (½ pint) **milk**
2 tablespoons **extra virgin olive oil**
**butter**, to serve

**Lightly** oil 8 muffin tin holes with spray oil. Sift the flour and salt into a bowl and stir in the cornmeal, 50 g (2 oz) of the cheese, the tomatoes and basil. Make a well in the centre.

**Beat** the egg, milk and oil together in a separate bowl or jug, pour into the well and stir together until just combined. The batter should remain a little lumpy.

**Divide** the batter between the prepared muffin holes and scatter over the remaining cheese. Bake in a preheated oven, 180°C (350°F), Gas Mark 4, for 20–25 minutes until risen and golden. Leave to cool in the tin for 5 minutes, then transfer to a wire rack to cool. Serve warm with butter.

**For olive & pine nut muffins**, replace the sun-dried tomatoes with 100 g (3½ oz) chopped pitted black olives and stir in 50 g (2 oz) pine nuts. Keep the basil or use chopped fresh thyme instead. Continue the recipe as above.

# pesto scrambled eggs

Serves **4**
Preparation time **5 minutes**
Cooking time **5 minutes**

**12 eggs**
100 ml (3½ fl oz) **single cream**
25 g (1 oz) **butter**
4 slices of **granary bread**, toasted
4 tablespoons **Pesto** (see page 86)
**salt and black pepper**

**Beat** the eggs, cream and a little salt and pepper together in a bowl. Melt the butter in a large, nonstick frying pan, add the egg mixture and stir over a low heat with a wooden spoon until cooked to your liking.

**Put** a slice of toast on each serving plate. Spoon a quarter of the scrambled eggs on to each slice of toast, make a small indent in the centre and add a tablespoonful of pesto. Serve immediately.

**For cheesy scrambled eggs**, stir 125 g (4 oz) diced soft goats' cheese and 2 tablespoons chopped parsley into the eggs just before serving, and omit the pesto.

# potato rösti with frazzled eggs

Serves **4**
Preparation time **15 minutes**
Cooking time **15 minutes**

750 g (1½ lb) **Desiree
    potatoes**, peeled
1 **onion**, thinly sliced
2 teaspoons chopped
    **rosemary**
4 tablespoons **olive oil**
4 large **eggs**
**salt and black pepper**
chopped **parsley**, to garnish

**Using** a box grater, coarsely grate the potatoes. Wrap in a clean tea towel and squeeze out the excess liquid over the sink. Transfer to a bowl and stir in the onion, rosemary and salt and pepper.

**Heat** half the oil in a large frying pan. Divide the potato mixture into quarters and spoon into 4 x 12 cm (5 inch) mounds in the pan, pressing down to form patties. Cook over a medium heat for 5 minutes on each side, transfer to warmed serving plates and keep warm in a moderate oven.

**Heat** the remaining oil in the frying pan for about 1 minute until very hot, add the eggs, 2 at a time, and fry until the whites are bubbly and crisp looking. Serve the eggs on the rösti, garnished with chopped parsley.

**For rösti with poached eggs**, bring a saucepan of lightly salted water to a simmer and add 1 tablespoon white vinegar. Crack an egg into a cup. Swirl the simmering water with a large spoon, gently drop the egg into the centre and cook for 2–3 minutes. Carefully remove with a slotted spoon. Repeat with the remaining eggs and finish as above.

# mixed mushrooms on toast

Serves **4**

Preparation time **10 minutes**

Cooking time **5 minutes**

25 g (1 oz) **butter**

3 tablespoons **extra virgin olive oil**, plus extra to serve

750 g (1½ lb) **mixed mushrooms**, such as oyster, shiitake, flat and button, trimmed and sliced

2 **garlic cloves**, crushed

1 tablespoon chopped **thyme**

grated rind and juice of 1 **lemon**

2 tablespoons chopped **parsley**

4 slices of **sourdough bread**

100 g (3½ oz) **mixed salad leaves**

**salt and black pepper**

fresh **Parmesan cheese shavings**, to serve

**Melt** the butter with the oil in a large frying pan. As soon as the butter stops foaming, add the mushrooms, garlic, thyme, lemon rind and salt and pepper and cook over a medium heat, stirring, for 4–5 minutes until tender. Scatter over the parsley and squeeze over a little lemon juice.

**Meanwhile,** toast the bread, then arrange it on serving plates.

**Top** the sourdough toast with an equal quantity of the salad leaves and mushrooms, and drizzle over a little more oil and lemon juice. Scatter with Parmesan shavings and serve immediately.

**For field mushrooms & Camembert on toast**, trim 8 large field mushrooms, brush with 2 tablespoons olive oil and cook under a preheated hot grill for 4–5 minutes on each side. Lightly toast 4 slices of sourdough bread, top with the mushrooms and arrange 2 slices of Camembert cheese over each one. Cook under the grill for 2–3 minutes until the cheese has melted then serve.

# pancakes with blueberry sauce

Serves **4–6**
Preparation time **10 minutes**
Cooking time **20 minutes**

15 g (½ oz) **butter**
150 g (5 oz) **self-raising flour**
1 teaspoon **bicarbonate of soda**
40 g (1½ oz) **caster sugar**
1 **egg**, beaten
350 ml (12 fl oz) **buttermilk**
**icing sugar**, for dusting
**Greek-style yogurt or crème fraîche**, to serve

**For the blueberry sauce**
250 g (8 oz) fresh **blueberries**
2 tablespoons **clear honey**
dash of **lemon juice**

**Heat** the blueberries with the honey and lemon juice in a small saucepan over a low heat for about 3 minutes until they release their juices. Keep warm.

**Melt** the butter in a separate small saucepan. Sift the flour and bicarbonate of soda into a bowl and stir in the caster sugar. Beat the egg and buttermilk together in a separate bowl or jug, then gradually whisk into the dry ingredients with the melted butter to make a smooth batter.

**Heat** a nonstick frying pan until hot. Drop in large spoonfuls of the batter and cook over a high heat for 3 minutes until bubbles appear on the surface. Flip the pancakes over and cook for a further minute. Remove and keep warm in a moderate oven. Repeat with the remaining batter.

**Serve** the pancakes topped with the blueberry sauce and Greek-style yogurt or crème fraîche, and dusted with icing sugar.

**For pancakes with spiced apple sauce**, replace the blueberries with 1 peeled, cored and chopped juicy dessert apple and use maple syrup instead of the honey, adding 1 teaspoon ground cinnamon, or to taste.

# honeyed ricotta with summer fruits

Serves **4**

Preparation time **10 minutes**

125 g (4 oz) fresh
 **raspberries**
2 teaspoons **rosewater**
250 g (8 oz) **ricotta cheese**
250 g (8 oz) fresh **mixed
 summer berries**
2 tablespoons **clear honey
 with honeycomb**
2 tablespoons **pumpkin
 seeds**, toasted
pinch of ground **cinnamon**

**Rub** the raspberries through a fine nylon sieve to purée and remove the pips, then mix with the rosewater. Alternatively, put the raspberries and rosewater in a food processor or blender and process to a purée, then sieve to remove the pips.

**Slice** the ricotta into wedges and arrange on serving plates with the berries. Drizzle over the honey and the raspberry purée, adding a little honeycomb, and serve scattered with the pumpkin seeds and cinnamon.

**For apricot purée** to serve with the summer fruits and ricotta, use chopped, stoned, ripe apricots instead of raspberries and orange flower water in place of the rosewater. Purée the apricots in a food processor or blender – there is no need to sieve the purée as it does not contain pips.

# spiced citrus croissants

Serves **2–4**
Preparation time **15 minutes**
Cooking time **5 minutes**

2 **oranges**
50 ml (2 fl oz) **soured cream**
2 small **ruby or pink grapefruit**
1 teaspoon ground **cinnamon**, plus extra for sprinkling
1 tablespoon **caster sugar**
4 **croissants**

**Grate** the rind of one of the oranges and stir into the soured cream in a bowl.

**Peel** the other orange, then cut the skin and white membrane off both oranges and the grapefruit. Working over a separate bowl to catch the juice, cut between the membranes to remove the segments. Mix the fruit segments and juice with the cinnamon and sugar in a small saucepan. Heat over a low heat for 1–2 minutes.

**Meanwhile**, put the croissants on a baking sheet and bake in a preheated oven, 200°C (400°F), Gas Mark 6, for 5 minutes, or until thoroughly heated and slightly toasted.

**Split** the toasted croissants lengthways and spoon the fruit mixture over the bottom halves. Top with a spoonful of the soured cream mixture and a sprinkling of cinnamon, and replace the top halves. Serve immediately.

**For summer strawberry cream croissants**, combine 250 g (8 oz) hulled halved strawberries with 150 ml (¼ pint) extra thick double cream or clotted cream and 1–2 tablespoons icing sugar, to taste. Drizzle over a little elderflower cordial and spoon into toasted croissants.

# triple chocolate muffins

Serves **6**

Preparation time **10 minutes**

Cooking time **15 minutes**

50 g (2 oz) **plain dark chocolate chips**

50 g (2 oz) **unsalted butter**

2 **eggs**

75 g (3 oz) **caster sugar**

75 g (3 oz) **self-raising flour**

25 g (1 oz) **cocoa powder**

25 g (1 oz) **white chocolate chips**

**Line** 6 bun tin holes with paper cases.

**Melt** the plain chocolate chips and butter together in a small saucepan over a low heat. Beat the eggs, sugar, flour and cocoa powder together in a bowl. Fold in the melted chocolate mixture and the white chocolate chips.

**Spoon** the mixture into the paper cases and bake in a preheated oven, 180°C (350°F), Gas Mark 4, for 12 minutes until risen and firm to the touch. Transfer to a wire rack to cool slightly. Serve warm.

**For chocolate walnut muffins**, replace the white chocolate chips with 100 g (3½ oz) roughly chopped walnuts. Continue the recipe as above. Finish the cooked muffins with a teaspoon of melted chocolate on top and a walnut half on each, if you like.

# starters & snacks

# haloumi with pomegranate salsa

Serves **4**
Preparation time **10 minutes**
Cooking time **5 minutes**

500 g (1 lb) **haloumi cheese**, sliced
1 tablespoon **clear honey**

**For the pomegranate salsa**
½ **pomegranate**
4 tablespoons **extra virgin olive oil**
2 tablespoons chopped **parsley**
1 tablespoon **lemon juice**
1 small **red chilli**, deseeded and finely chopped
1 small **garlic clove**, crushed
1 teaspoon **pomegranate syrup** (optional)
**salt and black pepper**

**First** make the pomegranate salsa. Carefully scoop the pomegranate seeds into a bowl, discarding all the white membrane. Stir in the remaining ingredients and season with salt and pepper.

**Heat** a large nonstick frying pan for 2–3 minutes until hot. Add the haloumi slices, in batches, and cook over a high heat for about 60 seconds on each side until browned and softened.

**Meanwhile**, warm the honey in a small saucepan until runny.

**Transfer** the pan-fried haloumi to serving plates and spoon over the salsa. Drizzle the honey over the haloumi and salsa, and serve immediately.

**For avocado salsa**, peel, stone and finely dice 1 small ripe avocado and combine with 4 finely chopped spring onions, 1 tablespoon lemon juice, 1 tablespoon chopped fresh coriander and salt and pepper to taste.

# sweetcorn & kaffir lime fritters

Serves **4**

Preparation time **20 minutes, plus cooling**

Cooking time **about 45 minutes**

275 g (9 oz) can **sweetcorn**, drained

65 g (2½ oz) **plain flour**

1 teaspoon **baking powder**

1 **egg**, lightly beaten

2 tablespoons **light soy sauce**

1½ tablespoons **lime juice**

4 **Kaffir lime leaves**, very finely shredded

1 tablespoon chopped **fresh coriander**

2 tablespoons **vegetable oil**

**For the chilli jam**

500 g (1 lb) ripe **tomatoes**

4 **red bird's eye chillies**

2 **garlic cloves**

2 tablespoons **dark soy sauce**

200 g (7 oz) **soft light brown sugar**

75 ml (3 fl oz) **rice wine vinegar**

½ teaspoon **salt**

**First** make the chilli jam. Roughly chop the tomatoes, chillies and garlic cloves, then put in a food processor and process until fairly smooth. Transfer to a saucepan and add the remaining ingredients. Bring to the boil, then reduce the heat and simmer gently, stirring occasionally to prevent the sauce sticking, for 30–40 minutes until thick and jam like. Set aside to cool completely.

**Put** half the sweetcorn in a food processor and process until fairly smooth. Sift in the flour and baking powder and add the egg, soy sauce and lime juice. Process again until combined and transfer to a bowl. Stir in the remaining sweetcorn, lime leaves and coriander.

**Heat** the oil in a large frying pan. Drop in 6 separate tablespoonfuls of the batter, pat them flat and fry over a medium-high heat for 1½ minutes on each side until cooked through. Repeat with the remaining batter to make 12 x 5 cm (2 inch) fritters. Serve the fritters hot with the chilli jam, garnished with lime wedges and coriander sprigs.

**For sweetcorn fritter wraps**, serve the fritters in lettuce cups, using 4 large iceberg or cos lettuce leaves. Add the chilli jam, wrap and serve. For a more substantial wrap, use wheat tortillas to wrap the fritters with shredded lettuce and the chilli jam.

# gnocchi with sage butter

Serves **4**

Preparation time **30 minutes**

Cooking time **15–18 minutes**

500 g (1 lb) **floury potatoes**, cubed

1 **egg**, beaten

1 teaspoon **sea salt**

2 tablespoons **olive oil**

175 g (6 oz) **plain flour**

125 g (4 oz) **butter**

2 tablespoons chopped **sage**

**salt**

freshly grated **Parmesan cheese**, to serve

**Cook** the potatoes in a saucepan of lightly salted boiling water for 10–12 minutes until tender. Drain, return the potatoes to the pan and heat gently for several seconds to dry out. Mash the potatoes and beat in the egg, salt, oil and flour to form a sticky dough.

**Take** walnut-sized pieces of the dough and roll into egg shapes, rolling them over the tines of a fork.

**Bring** a large saucepan of lightly salted water to a rolling boil, add half the gnocchi (freeze the remainder for later use) and cook for 3 minutes until they rise to the surface. Drain the gnocchi and transfer to serving bowls.

**Meanwhile**, melt the butter in a frying pan. As soon as it stops foaming, add the sage and fry over a medium-high heat, stirring, for 2–3 minutes until crisp and the butter turns golden brown. Drizzle over the gnocchi, scatter with grated Parmesan and serve immediately.

**For gnocchi, plum tomato & sage butter gratin**, follow the recipe above, but once the gnocchi is drained, spoon it into 4 individual gratin dishes and divide 8 quartered plum tomatoes equally between the dishes. Mix the tomatoes in with the gnocchi. Pour the sage butter over the gnocchi and scatter with grated Parmesan. Brown under a preheated hot grill for 1–2 minutes until golden.

# sweet potato & fontina panini

Serves **2–4**
Preparation time **10 minutes**
Cooking time **10–15 minutes**

250 g (8 oz) **sweet potato**,
   peeled and thinly sliced
1 tablespoon **extra virgin
   olive oil**
**vegetable oil**, for shallow-
   frying
12 **sage leaves**
1 **ciabatta**
2 tablespoons ready-made
   **olive tapenade**
250 g (8 oz) **fontina cheese**,
   thinly sliced
**salt and black pepper**

**Brush** the sweet potato slices with the olive oil and season lightly with salt and pepper. Heat a ridged griddle pan until hot. Add the sweet potato slices, in batches if necessary, and cook for 3–4 minutes on each side until charred and tender. Remove and set aside. Clean the griddle pan.

**Meanwhile**, heat a little vegetable oil in a small frying pan, add the sage leaves and fry over a medium-high heat, stirring, for 1–2 minutes until crisp. Remove and drain on kitchen paper.

**Cut** the ciabatta into quarters, then trim the quarters so that all 4 pieces will fit in the griddle pan. Heat the griddle pan and brush with a little vegetable oil. Add the ciabatta pieces, cut-side down, and cook for 1 minute, or until toasted and charred. Depending on the size of your griddle pan, you may have to toast the bread in 2 batches.

**Spread** the toasted sides of the ciabatta with the tapenade and sandwich together with layers of fontina, sage leaves and sweet potato slices.

**Add** the whole sandwiches to the griddle pan and cook for 1–2 minutes on each side until toasted and the cheese in the centre has melted. Serve immediately with a green salad.

**For aubergine & mozzarella panini**, use 1 large aubergine, sliced widthways into 5 mm (¼ inch) slices, instead of the sweet potato, and replace the fontina with mozzarella. Flavour with basil leaves, unfried, instead of sage. Continue the recipe as above.

# bruschetta with tomatoes & ricotta

Serves **4**
Preparation time **10 minutes**
Cooking time **15 minutes**

500 g (1 lb) **vine-ripened cherry tomatoes**
2 tablespoons **extra virgin olive oil**
4 large slices of **sourdough bread**
1 large **garlic clove**, peeled
350 g (11½ oz) **ricotta cheese**
½ quantity **Basil Oil** (see page 124)
**salt and black pepper**
**basil leaves**, to garnish

**Spread** the tomatoes out in a roasting tin, season with salt and pepper and drizzle with the extra virgin olive oil. Roast in a preheated oven, 220°C (425°F), Gas Mark 7, for 15 minutes.

**Meanwhile,** heat a ridged griddle pan until hot. Add the bread slices and cook until toasted and charred on both sides. Rub all over with the garlic clove.

**Top** each bruschetta with a slice of ricotta and the roasted tomatoes, and drizzle over the basil oil. Garnish with basil leaves.

**For bruschetta with fig, rocket & feta**, toast 4 slices of sourdough bread as in the recipe above and rub each slice with garlic. Combine 4 quartered fresh figs with 150 g (5 oz) crumbled feta cheese, a good handful of baby rocket leaves and some chopped mint. Arrange on the bruschetta and serve drizzled with extra virgin olive oil.

# crostini with pea & ricotta pesto

Serves **6**

Preparation time **10 minutes**, plus cooling

Cooking time **10 minutes**

1 small **French stick**, sliced

3 tablespoons **extra virgin olive oil**, plus extra to serve

250 g (8 oz) fresh or frozen shelled **peas**

1 small **garlic clove**, crushed

50 g (2 oz) **ricotta cheese**

juice of ½ **lemon**

1 tablespoon chopped **mint**

15 g (½ oz) **Parmesan cheese**, freshly grated

**salt and black pepper**

**Lay** the bread slices on a baking sheet, brush lightly with 1 tablespoon of the oil and bake in a preheated oven, 190°C (375°F), Gas Mark 5, for 5–6 minutes until crisp and golden. Leave to cool on a wire rack while you prepare the pesto.

**Cook** the peas in a saucepan of lightly salted boiling water for 3 minutes. Drain and immediately refresh under cold water. Put the peas in a food processor, add the remaining oil, the garlic, ricotta, lemon juice, mint, Parmesan and salt and pepper and process until fairly smooth.

**Spread** the crostini with the pesto and serve drizzled with oil.

**For broad bean & dill pesto**, replace the peas with 250 g (8 oz) frozen (or fresh shelled) broad beans and cook in a saucepan of lightly salted boiling water for 3 minutes. Drain well, refresh under cold water and continue as in the recipe above, replacing the mint with an equal amount of chopped dill.

# sage & goats' cheese frittata

Serves **4**
Preparation time **10 minutes**
Cooking time **10 minutes**

25 g (1 oz) **butter**, plus extra
   if necessary
18 large **sage leaves**
50 g (2 oz) **soft goats'**
   **cheese**, crumbled
2 tablespoons **crème fraîche**
4 **eggs**
**salt and black pepper**

**Melt** the butter in a nonstick frying pan. As soon as it stops foaming, add the sage leaves and fry over a medium-high heat, stirring, for 2–3 minutes until crisp and the butter turns golden brown. Take out 6 of the leaves and drain on kitchen paper. Transfer the remaining leaves and butter to a bowl.

**Beat** the goats' cheese and crème fraîche together in a separate bowl. Beat the eggs in another bowl, season with salt and pepper, then stir in the sage leaves with the butter.

**Reheat** the frying pan, adding a little extra butter if necessary. Pour in the egg mixture and dot over spoonfuls of the goats' cheese mixture. Cook over a medium heat for 4–5 minutes until the underside is set, then transfer to a preheated hot grill to brown the top lightly. Leave to cool slightly, then gently slide the frittata on to a serving plate. Garnish with the reserved sage leaves and serve with crusty bread.

**For spinach & goats' cheese frittata**, cook 175 g (6 oz) baby spinach leaves and 1 crushed garlic clove in the butter instead of the sage leaves for 2 minutes, or until the spinach has wilted. Stir into the beaten eggs at the second stage and continue with the recipe as above.

# baked figs with goats' cheese

Serves **4**

Preparation time **10 minutes**

Cooking time **10–12 minutes**

8 firm but ripe fresh **figs**

75 g (3 oz) **soft goats' cheese**

8 **mint leaves**

2 tablespoons **extra virgin olive oil**

**salt and black pepper**

**For the rocket salad**

150 g (5 oz) **baby rocket leaves**

1 tablespoon **extra virgin olive oil**

1 teaspoon **lemon juice**

**salt and black pepper**

**Cut** a cross in the top of each fig without cutting through the base. Put 1 teaspoonful of the goats' cheese and a mint leaf in each fig. Transfer to a roasting tin, then season with salt and pepper and drizzle with the oil. Bake in a preheated oven, 190°C (375°F), Gas Mark 5, for 10–12 minutes until the figs are soft and the cheese has melted.

**Put** the baby rocket leaves in a bowl. Whisk together the oil, lemon juice, salt and pepper and drizzle over the leaves. Serve with the figs.

**For figs stuffed with mozzarella & basil**, replace the goats' cheese with 125 g (4 oz) sliced mozzarella and use basil leaves instead of the mint leaves. Continue the recipe as above. Serve with sprigs of watercress instead of the rocket salad.

# tofu with chilli vinegar dressing

Serves **4**

Preparation time **15 minutes**, plus cooling

Cooking time **about 15 minutes**

**vegetable oil**, for deep-frying

500 g (1 lb) **silken tofu**, drained

50 g (2 oz) **cornflour**

2 teaspoons **salt**, plus extra to serve

1 teaspoon **Chinese five-spice powder**, plus extra to serve

**For the chilli vinegar dressing**

75 ml (3 fl oz) **rice wine vinegar**

75 ml (3 fl oz) **water**

2 tablespoons **caster sugar**

1 tablespoon **light soy sauce**

1 large **red chilli**, deseeded and finely chopped

1 teaspoon **sesame oil**

**First** make the dressing. Combine the vinegar, measurement water and sugar in a bowl and stir until the sugar has dissolved. Bring to the boil in a saucepan, then reduce the heat and simmer for 5–6 minutes until reduced by half and syrup like. Leave to cool for 30 minutes, then stir in the soy sauce, chilli and sesame oil. Pour into a serving bowl.

**Heat** 5 cm (2 inches) vegetable oil in a deep, heavy-based saucepan until it reaches 180–190°C (350–375°F), or until a cube of bread browns in 30 seconds. Meanwhile, cut the tofu into 3 cm (1¼ inch) cubes. Combine the cornflour, salt and Chinese five-spice powder in a bowl. Dip the tofu cubes, a few pieces at a time, in the cornflower mixture, add to the hot oil and deep-fry for 2–3 minutes until crisp and golden. Remove with a slotted spoon and drain on kitchen paper.

**Arrange** the tofu on a serving platter and dust with a little extra salt and Chinese five-spice powder. Serve with the chilli vinegar dressing for dipping.

**For roasted spiced tofu**, cut 500 g (1 lb) firm tofu into 2.5 cm (1 inch) cubes. Combine with 2 tablespoons soy sauce, 1 tablespoon sweet chilli sauce, 1 teaspoon clear honey and a pinch of Chinese five-spice powder. Spread out in a roasting tin and roast in a preheated oven, 220°C (425°F), Gas Mark 7, for 15–20 minutes until golden.

# aubergine dip with flatbreads

Serves **6**

Preparation time **15 minutes**, plus cooling

Cooking time **15 minutes**

1 large aubergine

4 tablespoons **extra virgin olive oil**

1 teaspoon ground **cumin**

150 ml (5 fl oz) **Greek-style yogurt**

1 small **garlic clove**, crushed

2 tablespoons chopped **fresh coriander**

1 tablespoon **lemon juice**

4 **flour tortillas**

**salt and black pepper**

**Cut** the aubergine lengthways into 5 mm (¼ inch) thick slices. Mix 3 tablespoons of the oil with the cumin and salt and pepper and brush all over the aubergine slices. Cook in a preheated ridged griddle pan or under a preheated hot grill for 3–4 minutes on each side until charred and tender. Leave to cool, then finely chop.

**Mix** the aubergine into the yogurt in a bowl, then stir in the garlic, coriander, lemon juice, the remaining oil and salt and pepper to taste. Transfer to a serving bowl.

**Cook** the tortillas in the preheated griddle pan or under the preheated hot grill for 3 minutes on each side until toasted. Cut into triangles and serve immediately with the aubergine dip.

**For cucumber & mint dip**, finely grate ½ cucumber and squeeze dry, then put in a bowl and stir in the remaining dip ingredients as above, replacing the coriander with an equal amount of chopped mint.

# felafel pitta pockets

Serves **4**
Preparation time **15 minutes**,
  plus soaking
Cooking time **12 minutes**

250 g (8 oz) **dried chickpeas**
1 small **onion**, finely chopped
2 **garlic cloves**, crushed
½ bunch of **parsley**
½ bunch **fresh coriander**
2 teaspoons **ground
  coriander**
½ teaspoon **baking powder**
**vegetable oil**, for shallow-
  frying
4 **pitta breads**
handful of **salad leaves**
2 **tomatoes**, diced
**Greek-style yogurt**, to serve

**Put** the dried chickpeas in a bowl, add cold water to cover by a generous 10 cm (4 inches) and leave to soak overnight.

**Drain** the chickpeas, transfer to a food processor and process until coarsely ground. Add the onion, garlic, herbs, ground coriander, baking powder and salt and pepper and process until really smooth. Using wet hands, shape the mixture into 16 small patties.

**Heat** a little vegetable oil in a large frying pan, add the patties, in batches, and fry over a medium-high heat for 3 minutes on each side until golden and cooked through. Remove and drain on kitchen paper.

**Split** the pitta breads and fill with the felafel, salad leaves and diced tomatoes. Add a spoonful of Greek-style yogurt and serve immediately.

**For felafel salad**, toss 4 handfuls of mixed salad leaves with a little extra virgin olive oil, lemon juice and salt and pepper, and arrange on serving plates. Core, deseed and dice 1 red pepper and sprinkle it over the salads. Top with the felafel and spoon over a little Tahini Yogurt Sauce (see page 76).

# pumpkin with walnut pesto

Serves **4**
Preparation time **15 minutes**
Cooking time **20–25 minutes**

1 kg (2 lb) **pumpkin**
**extra virgin olive oil**, for
  brushing
**salt and black pepper**

For the walnut pesto
50 g (2 oz) **walnuts**, toasted
2 **spring onions**, trimmed and
  chopped
1 large **garlic clove**, crushed
50 g (2 oz) **rocket leaves**,
  plus extra to serve
3 tablespoons **walnut oil**
3 tablespoons **extra virgin
  olive oil**

**Cut** the pumpkin into 8 wedges. Remove the seeds and fibre but leave the skin on. Brush all over with olive oil, season with salt and pepper and spread out on a large baking sheet. Roast in a preheated oven, 220°C (425°F), Gas Mark 7, for 20–25 minutes until tender, turning halfway through.

**Meanwhile**, make the pesto. Put the walnuts, spring onions, garlic and rocket in a food processor and process until finely chopped. With the motor running, gradually drizzle in the oils. Season the pesto with salt and pepper.

**Serve** the roasted pumpkin with the pesto and extra rocket leaves.

**For gnocchi with walnut pesto**, make the pesto as in the recipe above. Prepare and cook the gnocchi following the recipe on page 46 using half the amount for a starter or all the gnocchi for a main course. If you already have a half quantity of gnocchi in the freezer, cook it from frozen in a large saucepan of lightly salted boiling water for 5–6 minutes until the gnocchi rise to the surface, then drain, transfer to a buttered serving dish and top with the pesto.

# mushroom & ginger wontons

Serves **4**

Preparation time **30 minutes**, plus cooling

Cooking time **10–12 minutes**

2 tablespoons **vegetable oil**
1 **garlic clove**, crushed
1 teaspoon grated **fresh root ginger**
250 g (8 oz) **mixed mushrooms**, trimmed and finely chopped
1 tablespoon **dark soy sauce**
1 tablespoon chopped **fresh coriander**
16 **wonton wrappers**

**For the Szechuan chilli dressing**

1 teaspoon **dried chilli flakes**
150 ml (¼ pint) **vegetable stock**
1 tablespoon **rice wine vinegar**
1 tablespoon **light soy sauce**
2 teaspoons **caster sugar**
¼ teaspoon freshly ground **Szechuan pepper**

**Heat** the oil in a frying pan, add the garlic and ginger and cook over a medium heat, stirring, for 2–3 minutes. Add the mushrooms and soy sauce and cook, stirring, for 3–4 minutes until golden. Remove from the heat, season with salt and pepper and stir in the coriander. Leave to cool.

**Meanwhile**, make the dressing. Put all the ingredients in a saucepan and heat over a low heat, stirring, until hot but not boiling. Keep warm.

**Put** a teaspoon of the mushroom mixture in the centre of each wonton wrapper. Brush a little water around the filling and fold the wontons in half diagonally, pressing the edges together to seal.

**Bring** a large saucepan of lightly salted water to a rolling boil, add the wontons and cook for 2–3 minutes until they rise to the surface. Gently drain and transfer to warmed serving bowls. Strain over the dressing and serve immediately.

**For crispy mushroom wontons**, heat 5 cm (2 inches) vegetable oil in a wok or deep, heavy-based saucepan until it reaches 180–190°C (350–375°F), or until a cube of bread browns in 30 seconds. Add the wontons, in batches, and deep-fry for 2–3 minutes until crisp and golden. Remove with a slotted spoon and drain on kitchen paper. Serve with Chilli Jam (see page 44). Wonton wrappers are available fresh or frozen from Asian food stores.

# bean, lemon & rosemary hummus

Serves **4–6**

Preparation time **10 minutes**, plus cooling

Cooking time **10 minutes**

6 tablespoons **extra virgin olive oil**, plus extra to serve

4 **shallots**, finely chopped

2 large **garlic cloves**, crushed

1 teaspoon chopped **rosemary**, plus extra sprigs to garnish

grated rind and juice of ½ **lemon**

2 x 400 g (13 oz) cans **butter beans**

**salt and black pepper**

**toasted ciabatta**, to serve

**Heat** the oil in a frying pan, add the shallots, garlic, chopped rosemary and lemon rind and cook over a low heat, stirring occasionally, for 10 minutes until the shallots are softened. Leave to cool.

**Transfer** the shallot mixture to a food processor, add all the remaining ingredients and process until smooth.

**Spread** the hummus on to toasted ciabatta, garnish with rosemary sprigs and serve drizzled with oil.

**For chickpea & chilli hummus**, put 2 x 400 g (13 oz) cans drained chickpeas in a food processor with 2 deseeded and chopped red chillies, 1 large crushed garlic clove, 2 tablespoons lemon juice and salt and pepper to taste. Process with enough extra virgin olive oil to form a soft paste. Serve as a dip with vegetable crudités.

# onion, walnut & blue cheese tarts

Makes **8**
Preparation time **20 minutes**,
  plus cooling
Cooking time **35–40 minutes**

40 g (1½ oz) **butter**
500 g (1 lb) **onions**, thinly
  sliced
2 **garlic cloves**, crushed
1 tablespoon chopped **thyme**
50 g (2 oz) **walnuts**, chopped
350 g (11½ oz) **puff pastry**,
  defrosted if frozen
**plain flour**, for dusting
150 g (5 oz) **blue cheese**,
  diced
**salt and black pepper**

**Melt** the butter in a frying pan, add the onions, garlic and thyme and cook over a medium heat, stirring occasionally, for 20–25 minutes until soft and golden. Stir in the walnuts. Leave to cool.

**Roll** the pastry out on a lightly floured work surface to form a rectangle 40 x 20 cm (16 x 8 inches), trimming the edges. Cut the rectangle vertically in half, then cut horizontally into quarters to make eight 10 cm (4 inch) squares.

**Divide** the onion mixture between the squares, spreading over the surface but leaving a narrow border around the edges. Scatter over the blue cheese. Transfer the pastries to a large baking sheet and bake in a preheated oven, 220°C (425°F), Gas Mark 7, for 12–15 minutes until the pastry is puffed and the cheese is golden. Leave to cool slightly and serve warm.

**For onion & goats' cheese tart**, roll the pastry out but leave whole and lay on a baking sheet. Spread the onion mixture over the pastry, leaving a 1 cm (½ inch) border. Scatter over 200 g (7 oz) crumbled or diced soft goats' cheese and bake for 20–25 minutes until the pastry is puffed up and the cheese is golden.

# main
# meals

# butternut squash, tofu & pea curry

Serves **4**
Preparation time **15 minutes**
Cooking time **25 minutes**

1 tablespoon **sunflower oil**
1 tablespoon **Thai red curry paste**
500 g (1 lb) peeled, deseeded **butternut squash**, cubed
450 ml (¾ pint) **vegetable stock**
400 g (13 oz) can **coconut milk**
6 Kaffir **lime leaves**, bruised, plus extra shredded leaves to garnish
200 g (7 oz) **frozen peas**
300 g (10 oz) **firm tofu**, diced
2 tablespoons **light soy sauce**
juice of 1 **lime**
chopped **fresh coriander**, to garnish
finely chopped **red chilli**, to garnish

**Heat** the oil in a wok or deep frying pan, add the curry paste and stir-fry over a low heat for 1 minute. Add the squash, stir-fry briefly and then add the stock, coconut milk and the bruised lime leaves. Bring to the boil, then cover, reduce the heat and simmer gently for 15 minutes until the squash is cooked.

**Stir** in the peas, tofu, soy sauce and lime juice and simmer for a further 5 minutes until the peas are cooked. Spoon into serving bowls, garnish with shredded lime leaves and chopped coriander.

**For green vegetable curry**, use green curry paste instead of red curry paste. Replace the squash with 1 sliced carrot, 1 sliced courgette and 1 cored, deseeded and sliced red pepper and continue as in the recipe above.

# grilled vegetables & couscous

Serves **4**
Preparation time **20 minutes**
Cooking time **16–20 minutes**

1 large **aubergine**
2 large **courgettes**
2 **red peppers**, cored,
　deseeded and quartered
4 tablespoons **olive oil**
200 g (7 oz) **couscous**
450 ml (¾ pint) boiling
　**vegetable stock**
50 g (2 oz) **butter**
2 tablespoons chopped
　**mixed herbs**, such as mint,
　coriander and parsley
juice of **1 lemon**
**salt and black pepper**

**For the tahini yogurt sauce**
125 g (4 oz) **Greek-style**
　**yogurt**
1 tablespoon **tahini paste**
　(see page 13)
1 **garlic clove**, crushed
½ tablespoon **lemon juice**
1 tablespoon **extra virgin**
　**olive oil**

**Cut** the aubergine and courgettes into 5 mm (¼ inch) thick slices and put in a large bowl with the red peppers. Add the olive oil and salt and pepper and stir well.

**Heat** a ridged griddle pan until hot. Add the vegetables, in batches, and cook for 3–4 minutes on each side, depending on size, until charred and tender.

**Meanwhile**, prepare the couscous. Put the couscous in a heatproof bowl. Pour over the boiling stock, cover and leave to soak for 5 minutes. Fluff up the grains with a fork and stir in the butter, herbs, lemon juice and salt and pepper to taste.

**Make** the tahini yogurt sauce. Combine all the ingredients in a bowl and season with salt and pepper. Serve with the vegetables and couscous.

**For garlic mayonnaise** to serve instead of the tahini yogurt sauce, crush 1–2 garlic cloves and stir into 150 g (5 oz) good-quality mayonnaise. Serve with the vegetables and couscous.

# roasted stuffed peppers

Serves **2**
Preparation time **10 minutes**
Cooking time **55 minutes–
    1 hour**

4 large **red peppers**
2 **garlic cloves**, crushed
1 tablespoon chopped **thyme**,
    plus extra to garnish
4 **plum tomatoes**, halved
4 tablespoons **extra virgin
    olive oil**
2 tablespoons **balsamic
    vinegar**
**salt and black pepper**

**Cut** the red peppers in half lengthways, then scoop out and discard the cores and seeds. Put the pepper halves, cut-sides up, in a roasting tin lined with foil or a ceramic dish. Divide the garlic and thyme between them and season with salt and pepper.

**Put** a tomato half in each pepper and drizzle with the oil and vinegar. Roast in a preheated oven, 220°C (425°F), Gas Mark 7, for 55 minutes–1 hour until the peppers are soft and charred.

**Serve** with some crusty bread to mop up the juices and a baby leaf salad, if you like.

**For colourful, cheesy roasted peppers**, use a mixture of green, yellow and red peppers. After 45 minutes cooking time, top each pepper with a slice of mozzarella cheese and return to the oven for the remaining 10–15 minutes. Serve with wedges of wholemeal soda bread.

# creamy pea & mint risotto with brie

Serves **4**
Preparation time **15 minutes**
Cooking time **35 minutes**

1.2 litres (2 pints) **vegetable stock**
50 g (2 oz) **butter**
1 large **onion**, finely chopped
2 **garlic cloves**, crushed
300 g (10 oz) **arborio rice**
150 ml (¼ pint) **dry white wine**
350 g (11½ oz) fresh or frozen shelled **peas**
½ bunch fresh **mint leaves**, torn
50 g (2 oz) **Brie**, diced
**salt and black pepper**
freshly grated **Parmesan cheese**, to serve

**Put** the stock in a saucepan and bring to a very gentle simmer.

**Meanwhile**, melt the butter in a saucepan, add the onion, garlic and salt and pepper and cook over a low heat, stirring occasionally, for 10 minutes until the onion is softened but not browned. Add the rice and cook, stirring, for 1 minute until all the grains are glossy. Stir in the wine, bring to the boil and continue to boil for 1–2 minutes until absorbed. Stir in the peas.

**Stir** about 150 ml (¼ pint) of the stock into the rice. Cook over a medium heat, stirring constantly, until absorbed. Continue to add the stock, a little at a time, and cook, stirring constantly, for about 20 minutes until the rice is al dente and the stock has all been absorbed.

**Remove** the pan from the heat. Stir in the mint and Brie, cover and leave to stand for 5 minutes until the cheese has melted. Serve with grated Parmesan.

**For rice patties**, leave the risotto until completely cold, then stir in 1 beaten egg. Divide the mixture into small patties and coat with dried breadcrumbs. Heat a little vegetable oil in a frying pan, add the patties and fry for 2–3 minutes on each side until golden and cooked through. Serve with a green salad.

# broad bean & lemon spaghetti

Serves **4**
Preparation time **10 minutes**
Cooking time **15–18 minutes**

450 g (14½ oz) **dried
  spaghetti**
350 g (11½ oz) fresh or frozen
  shelled **broad beans**
4 tablespoons **extra virgin
  olive oil**
3 **garlic cloves**, finely
  chopped
pinch of **dried chilli flakes**
grated rind and juice of
  1 **lemon**
2 tablespoons torn **basil
  leaves**
**salt and black pepper**
freshly grated **Parmesan or
  pecorino cheese**, to serve
  (optional)

**Cook** the pasta in a large saucepan of lightly salted boiling water for 10–12 minutes, or according to the packet instructions, until al dente. Drain, reserving 4 tablespoons of the cooking water, and return the pasta to the pan.

**Meanwhile**, cook the beans in a separate saucepan of salted boiling water for 3–4 minutes. Drain well.

**While** the pasta and beans are cooking, heat the oil in a frying pan, add the garlic, chilli flakes, lemon rind and salt and pepper and cook over a low heat, stirring, for 3–4 minutes until the garlic is soft but not browned.

**Scrape** the oil mixture into the pasta with the beans, reserved pasta cooking water, lemon juice and basil and stir over a medium heat until heated through. Serve with grated Parmesan or pecorino.

**For spaghetti with peas & mint**, replace the broad beans with an equal quantity of shelled fresh peas and cook as in the recipe above, adding 2 tablespoons chopped mint instead of the basil just before serving. Frozen petit pois can be used instead of fresh peas.

# leek & thyme sausages with relish

Serves **4**

Preparation time **25 minutes**,
   plus soaking and cooling

Cooking time **45–50 minutes**

1 tablespoon **olive oil**

1 **leek**, trimmed and finely
   chopped

2 teaspoons chopped **thyme**

150 g (5 oz) **Cheddar
   cheese**, grated

150 g (5 oz) **fresh
   wholemeal breadcrumbs**

100 g (3½ oz) **ricotta cheese**

1 tablespoon **wholegrain
   mustard**

1 **egg**, beaten

50 g (2 oz) **dried white or
   wholemeal breadcrumbs**

**sunflower oil**, for shallow-
   frying

**salt and black pepper**

**For the relish**

2 tablespoons **olive oil**

2 **red onions**, thinly sliced

50 g (2 oz) **dried cranberries**

1 tablespoon **balsamic
   vinegar**

100 g (3½ oz) **cranberry
   sauce**

**First** make the relish. Heat the olive oil in a saucepan, add the onions and cook over a medium heat, stirring occasionally, for 20–25 minutes until soft and golden. Meanwhile, soak the cranberries in the vinegar. Add to the onions with the cranberry sauce and 2 tablespoons water and cook for 10 minutes until thickened and jam like. Season with salt and pepper and leave to cool.

**Meanwhile,** heat the olive oil in a frying pan, add the leek and thyme and cook over a medium heat, stirring frequently, for 5 minutes. Leave to cool.

**Combine** the leek mixture, Cheddar, fresh breadcrumbs, ricotta, mustard and salt and pepper in a bowl. Stir in the egg and mix together to form a soft dough. Shape into 12 sausages and roll each one in the dried breadcrumbs.

**Heat** a little sunflower oil in a frying pan, add the sausages and fry over a medium heat, turning frequently, for 10 minutes until golden and cooked through. Serve immediately with the relish.

**For leek & thyme burgers with blue cheese**, use finely crumbled Danish blue cheese instead of the Cheddar. Shape the sausage mixture into 8 patties, coat in dried breadcrumbs and shallow-fry as above. Serve in soft bread rolls with shredded lettuce and sliced tomatoes.

# aubergine toasties with pesto

Serves **4**
Preparation time **15 minutes**
Cooking time **8–20 minutes**

1 large **aubergine**
4 tablespoons **extra virgin olive oil**
4 slices **sourdough bread**
2 **beefsteak tomatoes,** thickly sliced
200 g (7 oz) **mozzarella cheese**, sliced
**salt and black pepper**

**For the pesto**
50 g (2 oz) **basil leaves**
1 **garlic clove**, crushed
4 tablespoons **pine nuts**
100 ml (3½ fl oz) **extra virgin olive oil**
2 tablespoons freshly grated **Parmesan cheese**

**First** make the pesto. Put the basil, garlic, pine nuts, oil and salt and pepper in a food processor and process until fairly smooth. Transfer to a bowl, stir in the Parmesan and adjust the seasoning. Set aside until required.

**Cut** the aubergines into 1 cm (½ inch) thick slices. Season the oil with salt and pepper and brush over the aubergine slices. Heat a ridged griddle pan until hot. Add the aubergine slices, in batches if necessary, and cook for 4–5 minutes on each side until charred and tender.

**Meanwhile**, grill the sourdough bread.

**Top** the grilled bread with an aubergine slice. Spread with the pesto. Top with tomato and mozzarella slices and more pesto. Cook under a preheated hot grill for 1–2 minutes until bubbling and golden.

**For aubergine buck rarebit**, arrange the aubergine slices on large toasted soft bread roll halves with the pesto, sliced tomatoes and mozzarella. Grill until brown. Top each with a poached egg and serve immediately.

# beetroot & goats' cheese risotto

Serves **4–6**
Preparation time **15 minutes**
Cooking time **35 minutes**

1.2 litres (2 pints) **vegetable
  stock**
350 g (11½ oz) **cooked
  beetroot**, diced
4 tablespoons **extra virgin
  olive oil**
1 **red onion**, finely chopped
2 **garlic cloves**, crushed
2 teaspoons chopped **thyme**,
  plus extra to garnish
300 g (10 oz) **arborio rice**
125 ml (4 fl oz) **red wine**
100 g (3½ oz) **soft goats'
  cheese**, diced
100 g (3½ oz) **pecan nuts**,
  toasted and chopped
**salt and black pepper**

**Put** the stock and any beetroot juices in a saucepan and bring to a very gentle simmer.

**Meanwhile**, heat the oil in a separate saucepan, add the onion, garlic, thyme and salt and pepper and cook over a low heat, stirring occasionally, for 10 minutes until the onion is softened but not browned. Add the rice and cook, stirring, for 1 minute until all the grains are glossy. Stir in the wine, bring to the boil and continue to boil for 1–2 minutes until absorbed. Stir in the beetroot.

**Stir** about 150 ml (¼ pint) of the stock into the rice. Cook over a medium heat, stirring constantly, until absorbed. Continue to add the stock, a little at a time, and cook, stirring constantly, for about 20 minutes until the rice is al dente and the stock has all been absorbed.

**Remove** the pan from the heat. Stir in the goats' cheese and pecan nuts, cover and leave to stand for 2–3 minutes until the cheese has melted. Serve with a rocket salad.

### For beetroot & mascarpone risotto with pine nuts, replace the goats' cheese with 150 g (5 oz) mascarpone cheese. Sprinkle the risotto with pine nuts (about 1 tablespoon per portion) instead of adding pecan nuts. Vacuum-packed cooked beetroot is available from most supermarkets and is the best type (other than freshly cooked) to use for this recipe.

# spinach & mushroom lasagne

Serves **6–8**

Preparation time **35 minutes**, plus infusing

Cooking time **45–50 minutes**

4 tablespoons **olive oil**

2 **garlic cloves**, crushed

2 teaspoons chopped **thyme**

500 g (1 lb) **button mushrooms**, trimmed and sliced

500 g (1 lb) frozen **leaf spinach**, defrosted

**spray oil**, for oiling

200 g (7 oz) fresh **lasagne sheets**

**salt and black pepper**

**For the cheese sauce**

1.2 litres (2 pints) **milk**

2 fresh **bay leaves**

50 g (2 oz) **unsalted butter**, plus extra for greasing

50 g (2 oz) **plain flour**

250 g (8 oz) **Cheddar cheese**, grated

**First** make the sauce. Put the milk and bay leaves in a saucepan and heat to boiling point. Remove from the heat and leave to infuse for 20 minutes. Discard the bay leaves.

**Melt** the butter in a separate saucepan, add the flour and cook over a medium heat, stirring constantly, for 1 minute. Gradually stir in the milk and continue to cook, stirring, until the mixture boils. Reduce the heat and simmer for 2 minutes. Remove from the heat, add most of the Cheddar and stir until melted.

**Meanwhile,** heat the oil in a frying pan, add the garlic, thyme, mushrooms and salt and pepper and cook over a medium heat, stirring frequently, for 5 minutes until tender. Squeeze out the excess water from the spinach and roughly chop. Stir into the mushroom mixture. Remove from the heat.

**Lightly** oil a 2.5 litre (4 pint) lasagne dish with spray oil. Spread a quarter of the cheese sauce over the base and add one-third of the mushroom and spinach mixture and a lasagne sheet. Repeat these layers twice more. Add a final layer of sauce to cover the lasagne and scatter over the remaining cheese. Bake in a preheated oven, 190°C (375°F), Gas Mark 5, for 35–40 minutes until browned.

**For mushroom, flageolet & tomato lasagne**, replace the spinach with a tomato sauce (see page 186). Add a drained 425 g (14 oz) can flageolet beans to the mushroom mixture and layer with the tomato sauce, lasagne sheets and cheese sauce, and bake as the above recipe.

# omelette with basil tomatoes

Serves **4**
Preparation time **10 minutes**
Cooking time **16–20 minutes**

4 tablespoons **extra virgin olive oil**
500 g (1 lb) **cherry tomatoes**, halved
a few chopped **basil leaves**
12 **eggs**
2 tablespoons **wholegrain mustard**
50 g (2 oz) **butter**
100 g (3½ oz) **soft goats' cheese**, diced
**salt and black pepper**
**watercress**, to garnish

**Heat** the oil in a large frying pan, add the tomatoes, in batches if necessary, and cook, stirring gently, for 2–3 minutes until softened. Add the basil and season with salt and pepper. Transfer to a bowl and keep warm in a moderate oven.

**Beat** the eggs, mustard and salt and pepper together in a separate bowl. Melt a quarter of the butter in an omelette pan or small frying pan. As soon as it stops foaming, swirl in a quarter of the egg mixture and cook over a medium heat, forking over the omelette so that it cooks evenly.

**Dot** a quarter of the goats' cheese over one half of the omelette as soon as it is set on the underside, but still a little runny in the centre, and cook for a further 30 seconds. Carefully slide the omelette on to a warmed serving plate, folding it in half as you go. Keep warm in the oven. Repeat with the remaining egg mixture to make 3 more omelettes.

**Garnish** the omelettes with watercress and serve with the tomatoes and a green salad.

**For tomato stuffed omelette**, omit the first step of the above recipe. Arrange a quarter of the tomatoes with the goats' cheese over one half of the omelette as soon as it is set on the underside. Follow the recipe above to finish the omelette and then serve with a rocket salad.

# vegetable kebabs with pilaf

Serves **4**
Preparation time **20 minutes**,
  plus marinating and standing
Cooking time **25 minutes**

1 tablespoon chopped
  **rosemary**
5 tablespoons **extra virgin
  olive oil**
2 **courgettes**
1 large **red pepper**, cored and
  deseeded
16 **button mushrooms**,
  trimmed
8 **cherry tomatoes**
**Greek-style yogurt**, to serve

**For the pilaf**
250 g (8 oz) **basmati rice**
1 **onion**, finely chopped
2 **garlic cloves**, finely
  chopped
6 **cardamom pods**, bruised
100 g (3½ oz) **dried
  cranberries**
50 g (2 oz) **pistachio nuts**,
  toasted and chopped
2 tablespoons chopped **fresh
  coriander**
**salt and black pepper**

**Combine** the rosemary with 2 tablespoons of the oil and salt and pepper in a large bowl. Cut the courgettes and red pepper into large pieces, add to the oil with the mushrooms and tomatoes and toss well. Cover and leave to marinate for 20 minutes.

**Wash** the rice under cold water, drain and put in a saucepan. Add lightly salted water to cover the rice by at least 5 cm (2 inches). Bring to the boil and boil for 10 minutes. Drain well.

**Heat** the remaining oil in a separate saucepan, add the onion, garlic and cardamom pods and cook over a medium heat, stirring frequently, for 5 minutes until lightly golden. Add the rice, cranberries, pistachio nuts, coriander and salt and pepper. Stir well, then remove from the heat, cover and leave to stand for 10 minutes.

**Meanwhile,** heat a ridged griddle pan until hot. Thread the vegetables alternately on to 8 wooden skewers, presoaked in cold water for 30 minutes. Add to the pan and cook, turning frequently, for 10 minutes until all the vegetables are tender. Serve with the rice and Greek-style yogurt.

**For mixed spice pilaf**, boil the rice as above, adding ¼ teaspoon saffron threads to the water. Cook 1 chopped onion, 2 crushed garlic cloves, 1 cinnamon stick and 6 whole cloves in 50 g (2 oz) butter for 5 minutes in a saucepan. Add the freshly cooked rice and stir lightly. Remove from the heat, cover and leave to stand for 10 minutes.

# asian-style risotto

Serves **4**
Preparation time **15 minutes**
Cooking time **25 minutes**

1.2 litres (2 pints) **vegetable
  stock**
1 tablespoon **dark soy sauce**
2 tablespoons **mirin**
3 tablespoons **sunflower oil**
1 tablespoon **sesame oil**
1 bunch of **spring onions**,
  thickly sliced
2 **garlic cloves**, chopped
2.5 cm (1 inch) piece of **fresh
  root ginger**, peeled and
  grated
375 g (12 oz) **arborio rice**
6 **Kaffir lime leaves**
250 g (8 oz) **shiitake
  mushrooms**
15 g (½ oz) chopped **fresh
  coriander**, plus extra sprigs
  to garnish

**Put** the stock, soy sauce and mirin into a saucepan and bring to a very gentle simmer.

**Meanwhile**, heat 2 tablespoons of the sunflower oil and the sesame oil in a separate saucepan, add the spring onions, garlic and ginger and cook over a high heat, stirring, for 1 minute. Add the rice and lime leaves and cook over a low heat, stirring, for 1 minute until all the grains are glossy.

**Stir** about 150 ml (¼ pint) of the stock into the rice. Cook over a medium heat, stirring constantly, until absorbed. Continue to add the stock, a little at a time, and cook, stirring constantly, until all but a ladleful of stock has been absorbed.

**While the risotto is cooking**, wipe the mushrooms, discard the stalks and thinly slice all but a few. Heat the remaining oil in a frying pan, add all the mushrooms and cook over a medium heat, stirring frequently, for 5 minutes until golden.

**Add** the coriander to the risotto with the sliced mushrooms and the remaining stock. Cook, stirring, until the stock has been absorbed and the rice is al dente. Serve garnished with the reserved whole mushrooms and coriander sprigs.

**For Italian-style risotto**, omit the soy sauce, mirin, sesame oil and ginger, and use flat mushrooms instead of shiitake. Stir in 100 g (3½ oz) mascarpone and 4 tablespoons grated Parmesan at the end of cooking and leave to sit for 5 minutes before serving.

# stir-fried tofu with basil & chilli

Serves **4**

Preparation time **20 minutes**

Cooking time **6 minutes**

2 tablespoons **sunflower oil**

350 g (11½ oz) **firm tofu**, cubed

5 cm (2 inch) piece of **fresh root ginger**, shredded

2 **garlic cloves**, chopped

250 g (8 oz) **broccoli**, trimmed

250 g (8 oz) **sugar snap peas**, trimmed

150 ml (¼ pint) **vegetable stock**

2 tablespoons **sweet chilli sauce**

1 tablespoon **light soy sauce**

1 tablespoon **dark soy sauce**

1 tablespoon **lime juice**

2 teaspoons **soft light brown sugar**

handful of **Thai basil leaves**

**Heat** half the oil in a wok or deep frying pan until smoking, add the tofu and stir-fry for 2–3 minutes until golden all over. Remove with a slotted spoon.

**Add** the remaining oil to the pan, add the ginger and garlic and stir-fry for 10 seconds, then add the broccoli and sugar snap peas and stir-fry for 1 minute.

**Return** the tofu to the pan and add the stock, chilli sauce, soy sauces, lime juice and sugar. Cook for 1 minute until the vegetables are cooked but still crisp. Add the basil leaves and stir well. Serve immediately with rice or noodles.

**For tofu & vegetables in oyster sauce**, cook the tofu and vegetables as in the recipe above. Return the tofu to the pan and add 50 ml (2 fl oz) water, cook for 1 minute, then add 75 ml (3 fl oz) oyster sauce and heat through for a further minute. Omit the basil and garnish with chopped fresh coriander.

# spinach & ricotta cannelloni

Serves **4**

Preparation time **25 minutes**

Cooking time **35 minutes**

500 g (1 lb) frozen **leaf spinach**, defrosted

300 g (10 oz) **ricotta cheese**

1 **garlic clove**, crushed

2 tablespoons **single cream**

pinch of freshly grated **nutmeg**

16 **dried cannelloni tubes**

**spray oil**, for oiling

25 g (1 oz) **Parmesan cheese**, freshly grated

**salt and black pepper**

**For the tomato salsa**

500 g (1 lb) ripe **tomatoes**, diced

1 **garlic clove**, crushed

75 g (3 oz) pitted **black olives**, chopped

2 tablespoons **capers** in brine, drained

1 tablespoon chopped **parsley**

2 tablespoons **extra virgin olive oil**

**Squeeze** the excess water from the spinach and put in a bowl. Add the ricotta, garlic, cream, nutmeg and salt and pepper, and stir together until evenly combined.

**Cook** the cannelloni tubes in a large saucepan of boiling water for 5 minutes, or until just al dente. Drain well and immediately refresh under cold water. Pat dry with kitchen paper.

**Lightly** oil 4 individual gratin dishes with spray oil. Cut down one side of each cannelloni tube and open out flat. Spoon 2 tablespoons of the spinach and ricotta mixture down one side and roll the pasta up to form tubes once more. Divide between the prepared dishes.

**Combine** all the salsa ingredients in a bowl, then spoon over the cannelloni. Scatter with the Parmesan. Cover the dishes with foil and bake in a preheated oven, 200°C (400°F), Gas Mark 6, for 20 minutes. Remove the foil and bake for a further 10 minutes until bubbling and golden. Serve immediately.

**For pumpkin & ricotta cannelloni**, steam 500 g (1 lb) peeled, deseeded and finely diced pumpkin flesh for 10–12 minutes until tender. Leave to cool completely before mixing with the ricotta and other filling ingredients. Continue the recipe as above.

# asparagus, tomato & feta frittata

Serves **4**

Preparation time **10 minutes**,
  plus cooling

Cooking time **about
  40 minutes**

3 tablespoons **olive oil**, plus
  extra for oiling
2 **leeks**, thinly sliced
1 **garlic clove**, crushed
250 g (8 oz) **asparagus**,
  trimmed
6 **eggs**
100 g (3½ oz) **feta cheese**,
  diced
4 tablespoons freshly grated
  **Parmesan cheese**
175 g (6 oz) **cherry
  tomatoes**
**salt and black pepper**

**Heat** the oil in a frying pan, add the leeks and garlic
and cook over a medium heat, stirring frequently, for
10 minutes until tender. Leave to cool.

**Cook** the asparagus in a large saucepan of lightly
salted boiling water for 2 minutes. Drain, refresh under
cold water and pat dry. Cut into 5 cm (2 inch) lengths.

**Lightly** oil a 20 cm (8 inch) square baking dish with
olive oil and line the base with nonstick baking paper.
Beat the eggs in a bowl and stir in the leek mixture,
asparagus, feta, half the Parmesan and salt and
pepper. Pour the mixture into the prepared dish and
top with the tomatoes. Sprinkle over the remaining
Parmesan and bake in a preheated oven, 190°C
(375°F), Gas Mark 5, for 25–30 minutes until puffed
up and firm in the centre.

**Leave** to cool in the dish for 10 minutes, then turn out
on to a board and serve warm with a crisp green salad.

**For mixed mushroom frittata**, cook the leeks and
garlic as above with 2 teaspoons chopped thyme.
Add 350 g (11½ oz) sliced button mushrooms and
cook for a further 5 minutes. Omit the asparagus
and stir the mushrooms into 6 beaten eggs with
50 g (2 oz) grated Parmesan, 2 tablespoons chopped
parsley and salt and pepper. Bake as above.

# potato, chickpea & cashew curry

Serves **4–6**
Preparation time **20 minutes**
Cooking time **1 hour**

4 tablespoons **vegetable oil**
1 **onion**, sliced
2 **garlic cloves**, crushed
2 teaspoons grated **fresh root ginger**
2 teaspoons ground **coriander**
1 teaspoon ground **cumin**
½ teaspoon ground **turmeric**
½ teaspoon ground **cinnamon**
¼–½ teaspoon **chilli powder**
4 ripe **tomatoes**, chopped
300 ml (½ pint) **water**
500 g (1 lb) **potatoes**, cubed
400 g (13 oz) can **chickpeas**, drained
250 g (8 oz) **button mushrooms**, trimmed
75 g (3 oz) **unsalted cashew nuts**
2 tablespoons chopped **fresh coriander**
150 ml (¼ pint) **natural yogurt**
**salt and black pepper**

**Heat** half the oil in a large saucepan, add the onion, garlic, ginger, spices and salt and pepper and cook over a low heat, stirring occasionally, for 10 minutes until the onion is softened.

**Add** the tomatoes and measurement water to the pan and bring to the boil, then reduce the heat, cover and simmer for 15 minutes. Add the potatoes and chickpeas, cover and cook for 20 minutes.

**Meanwhile,** heat the remaining oil in a frying pan, add the mushrooms and cook over a medium heat, stirring frequently, for 3–4 minutes until browned.

**Add** the mushrooms to the curry with the cashew nuts and fresh coriander and cook for a further 10 minutes. Stir in the yogurt and heat through without boiling. Serve with rice.

**For aubergine & tomato curry**, cook the onion, garlic, ginger and spices as above and stir in a 400 g (13 oz) can chopped tomatoes. Meanwhile, heat 3 tablespoons vegetable oil in a large frying pan, add 1 large diced aubergine and cook over a medium heat, stirring frequently, for 5–6 minutes until golden. Stir into the sauce with the chickpeas and continue as in the recipe above.

# onion, pumpkin & sage pie

Serves **8**

Preparation time **25 minutes**, plus cooling

Cooking time **45–55 minutes**

50 g (2 oz) **butter**

750 g (1½ lb) **onions**, thinly sliced

2 **garlic cloves**, chopped

1 tablespoon chopped **sage**

1 kg (2 lb) **pumpkin**, peeled and deseeded

1 tablespoon **olive oil**

2 x 350 g (11½ oz) blocks of **puff pastry**, defrosted if frozen

**plain flour**, for dusting

250 g (8 oz) **fontina cheese**, sliced

1 **egg**, beaten

**salt and black pepper**

**Melt** the butter in a frying pan, add the onions, garlic, sage and salt and pepper and cook over a medium heat, stirring occasionally, for 20–25 minutes until soft and golden. Leave to cool.

**Meanwhile**, cut the pumpkin into 5 mm (¼ inch) thick slices and brush with the oil. Heat a ridged griddle pan until hot. Add the pumpkin, in batches, and cook for 2–3 minutes on each side until tender. Leave to cool.

**Roll** one pastry block out on a lightly floured work surface to form a rectangle a little smaller than a baking sheet. Lay on the sheet. Spread over half the onion mixture, leaving a 2.5 cm (1 inch) border. Top with half the pumpkin and half the cheese. Repeat these layers, seasoning with salt and pepper.

**Roll** out the remaining pastry a little larger than the first. Brush around the filling with beaten egg and top with the second piece of pastry. Press the edges together to seal, then decorate with the tines of a fork. Brush with beaten egg and score the surface with slashes.

**Bake** in a preheated oven, 220°C (425°F), Gas Mark 7, for 25–30 minutes until puffed and golden. Leave to cool slightly, then cut into slices and serve warm.

**For pumpkin filo pie**, layer 4 sheets of filo pastry into a 20 x 30 cm (8 x 12 inch) baking tin, brushing each with melted butter as you layer. Layer with the ingredients as above, then top with another 4 sheets of filo pastry, trimmed to fit the tin, brushing each with butter. Bake for 30 minutes until golden.

# soups & stews

# curried carrot & lentil soup

Serves **4**
Preparation time **15 minutes**
Cooking time **35 minutes**

2 tablespoons **olive oil**
1 **onion**, chopped
1 **garlic clove**, crushed
500 g (1 lb) **carrots**, chopped
1 **potato**, chopped
1 tablespoon **medium curry paste**
150 g (5 oz) **red split lentils**, washed
1 litre (1¾ pints) **vegetable stock**
1 tablespoon chopped **fresh coriander**
**salt and black pepper**

**For the lime oil**
4 tablespoons **extra virgin olive oil**
grated rind and juice of **1 lime**

**Heat** the oil in a saucepan, add the onion and garlic and cook over a medium heat, stirring frequently, for 5 minutes. Add the carrots, potato and curry paste, stir well and then add the remaining ingredients. Bring to the boil, then reduce the heat, cover and simmer gently for 25 minutes.

**Transfer** to a food processor or blender and process until really smooth. Return to the pan and heat through.

**Meanwhile**, make the lime oil. Whisk the ingredients together in a bowl until combined.

**Spoon** the soup into serving bowls, drizzle over the lime oil and serve with crusty bread rolls.

**For spiced carrot & tomato soup**, replace the potato with a 400 g (13 oz) can chopped tomatoes and add to the soup with the lentils. Stir in ½ teaspoon sugar, then continue as in the recipe above.

# mushroom soup with truffle butter

Serves **6**

Preparation time **15 minutes**, plus chilling and soaking

Cooking time **40 minutes**

1 tablespoon **dried porcini mushrooms**

4 tablespoons **boiling water**

75 g (3 oz) **butter**

2 **onions**, chopped

2 **garlic cloves**, crushed

2 tablespoons chopped **thyme**

1 kg (2 lb) **flat mushrooms**, trimmed and chopped

1 litre (1¾ pints) **vegetable stock**

250 ml (8 fl oz) **single cream**, plus extra to serve

**salt and black pepper**

chopped **chives**, to garnish

**For the truffle butter**

150 g (5 oz) **butter**, softened

2 teaspoons **truffle paste**

**First** make the truffle butter. Beat the butter and truffle paste together in a bowl until smooth. Form into a log, wrap in clingfilm and chill in the freezer for 30 minutes. Cut into slices.

**Meanwhile**, soak the porcini mushrooms in the measurement water for 15 minutes. Drain well, reserving the soaking liquid, then chop the porcini.

**Melt** half the butter in a saucepan, add the onions, garlic and thyme and cook over a low heat, stirring occasionally, for 10 minutes. Add the remaining butter and the fresh mushrooms and porcini and cook over a medium heat, stirring frequently, for 5 minutes, until the mushrooms are softened. Stir in the stock and the reserved soaking liquid and bring to the boil, then reduce the heat, cover and simmer gently for 20 minutes.

**Transfer** to a food processor or blender and process until really smooth. Return to the pan, stir in the cream and heat through without boiling. Spoon the soup into serving bowls and serve each portion topped with slices of the truffle butter and chopped chives.

**For mushroom, walnut & thyme soup**, replace the cream with milk and omit the truffle butter. Blend the cooked soup, spoon into bowls and serve drizzled with a little walnut oil. Garnish with a few thyme sprigs and finely chopped walnuts.

# chilli bean soup

Serves **3–4**
Preparation time **10 minutes**
Cooking time **25 minutes**

2 tablespoons **olive oil**
1 **onion**, chopped
1 **garlic clove**, crushed
1 teaspoon **hot chilli powder**
1 teaspoon ground
   **coriander**
½ teaspoon ground **cumin**
400 g (13 oz) can **red
   kidney beans**, drained
400 g (13 oz) can **chopped
   tomatoes**
600 ml (1 pint) **vegetable
   stock**
12 **tortilla chips**
50 g (2 oz) **Cheddar cheese**,
   grated
**salt and black pepper**
**soured cream**, to serve

**Heat** the oil in a saucepan, add the onion, garlic, chilli powder, coriander and cumin and cook over a medium heat, stirring frequently, for 5 minutes until the onion is softened. Add the beans, tomatoes and stock and season with salt and pepper. Bring to the boil, then reduce the heat, cover and simmer for 15 minutes.

**Transfer** to a food processor or blender and process until fairly smooth. Pour into flameproof bowls.

**Scatter** the tortilla chips on top of the soup and sprinkle over the Cheddar. Cook under a preheated hot grill for 1–2 minutes until the cheese has melted. Serve immediately with soured cream.

**For chilli bean soup with low-fat topping**, omit the tortilla chip and cheese topping. Split 3 pitta breads and cook under a preheated hot grill until toasted on both sides. Leave to cool slightly, then cut into triangles with kitchen scissors. Serve with the soup, together with a swirl of low-fat natural yogurt instead of the soured cream.

# pumpkin soup with olive salsa

Serves **6**
Preparation time **20 minutes**
Cooking time **40 minutes**

4 tablespoons **olive oil**
1 **large onion**, chopped
2 **garlic cloves**, crushed
1 tablespoon chopped **sage**
1 kg (2 lb) peeled,
  deseeded **pumpkin**, cubed
400 g (13 oz) can **cannellini
  or haricot beans**, drained
1 litre (1¾ pints) **vegetable
  stock**
**salt and black pepper**

**For the olive salsa**
100 g (3½ oz) pitted **black
  olives**
3 tablespoons **extra virgin
  olive oil**
grated rind of **1 lemon**
2 tablespoons chopped
  **parsley**

**Heat** the oil in a saucepan, add the onion, garlic and sage and cook over a low heat, stirring frequently, for 5 minutes. Add the pumpkin and beans and stir well, then add the stock and a little salt and pepper.

**Bring** to the boil, then reduce the heat, cover and simmer gently for 30 minutes until the pumpkin is tender. Transfer the soup to a food processor or blender and process until smooth. Return to the pan, adjust the seasoning and heat through.

**Meanwhile,** make the salsa. Chop the olives and mix with the oil, lemon rind, parsley and salt and pepper in a bowl.

**Serve** the soup in warmed bowls, topped with spoonfuls of the salsa.

**For roasted butternut squash soup**, use the same weight of butternut squash instead of pumpkin. Toss the cubes of butternut squash with 1 tablespoon olive oil and roast in a preheated oven, 200°C (400°F), Gas Mark 6, for 30 minutes until golden and tender. Continue with the recipe as above, but cook the soup for just 15 minutes.

# pea, potato & rocket soup

Serves **4–6**
Preparation time **15 minutes**
Cooking time **35 minutes**

3 tablespoons **extra virgin
olive oil**, plus extra to serve
1 **onion**, finely chopped
2 **garlic cloves**, finely
chopped
2 teaspoons chopped **thyme**
250 g (8 oz) **potatoes**,
chopped
500 g (1 lb) frozen or fresh
shelled **peas**
1 litre (1¾ pints) **vegetable
stock**
100 g (3½ oz) **rocket leaves**,
roughly chopped
juice of 1 **lemon**
**salt and black pepper**

**Heat** the oil in a saucepan, add the onion, garlic and
thyme and cook over a low heat, stirring frequently, for
5 minutes until the onion is softened. Add the potatoes
and cook, stirring frequently, for 5 minutes.

**Stir** in the peas, stock and salt and pepper. Bring to the
boil, then reduce the heat, cover and simmer gently for
20 minutes.

**Transfer** the soup to a food processor or blender,
add the rocket and lemon juice and process until
smooth. Return to the pan, adjust the seasoning and
heat through. Serve immediately, drizzled with a little
extra oil.

**For summer pea & asparagus soup**, omit the
potatoes and add 250 g (8 oz) asparagus spears.
Trim off the tips and cook them in the stock for
3–5 minutes, until tender. Drain and set aside,
reserving the stock. Slice the remaining asparagus
and add to the soup with the peas. Serve garnished
with the tips.

# winter vegetable & beer broth

Serves **6**

Preparation time **20 minutes**

Cooking time **50–55 minutes**

4 tablespoons **olive oil**

1 **onion**, chopped

2 **garlic cloves**, crushed

1 tablespoon chopped
   **rosemary**

2 **carrots**, diced

250 g (8 oz) **parsnips**, diced

250 g (8 oz) **swede**, diced

100 g (3½ oz) **pearl barley**

600 ml (1 pint) **beer or lager**

1 litre (1¾ pints) **vegetable
   stock**

2 tablespoons chopped
   **parsley**

**salt and black pepper**

**Heat** the oil in a large saucepan, add the onion, garlic, rosemary, carrots, parsnips and swede and cook over a low heat, stirring frequently, for 10 minutes.

**Stir** in the barley, beer or lager, stock and salt and pepper and bring to the boil. Reduce the heat, cover and simmer gently for 40–45 minutes until the barley and vegetables are tender. Stir in the parsley and adjust the seasoning. Serve with plenty of crusty bread.

**For vegetable & rice soup**, omit the beer and increase the stock to 1.5 litres (2½ pints). Replace the barley with an equal quantity of risotto rice. Use 250 g (8 oz) celeriac instead of the parsnips. Continue the recipe as above. Serve the soup garnished with some more chopped parsley and cracked black pepper.

# sweet potato & coconut soup

Serves **4**
Preparation time **15 minutes**
Cooking time **30 minutes**

2 tablespoons **olive oil**
1 **onion**, finely chopped
2 **garlic cloves**, crushed
1 teaspoon grated **fresh root
  ginger**
grated rind and juice of
  **1 lime**
1 **red chilli**, deseeded and
  chopped
750 g (1½ lb) **sweet
  potatoes**, peeled and
  roughly chopped
600 ml (1 pint) **vegetable
  stock**
400 g (13 oz) can **coconut
  milk**
150 g (5 oz) **baby spinach
  leaves**
**salt and black pepper**

**Heat** the oil in a saucepan, add the onion, garlic, ginger, lime rind and chilli and cook over a low heat, stirring frequently, for 5 minutes until the onion is softened. Add the sweet potatoes and cook, stirring frequently, for 5 minutes.

**Stir** in the stock, coconut milk, lime juice and salt and pepper. Bring to the boil, then reduce the heat, cover and simmer gently for 15 minutes, or until the potatoes are tender.

**Transfer** half the soup to a food processor or blender and process until smooth. Return to the pan, stir in the spinach and cook until just wilted. Adjust the seasoning and serve immediately.

### For creamy pumpkin, coriander & coconut soup,
replace the sweet potato with an equal quantity of peeled, deseeded and diced pumpkin. Cook the soup for 20 minutes, then process in a food processor or blender until smooth, adding 2 tablespoons chopped fresh coriander instead of the spinach. Finish the recipe as above.

# pasta & bean soup with basil oil

Serves **6**
Preparation time **15 minutes**
Cooking time **35 minutes**

2 tablespoons **extra virgin olive oil**
1 **onion**, chopped
3 **garlic cloves**, crushed
1 tablespoon chopped **rosemary**
2 x 400 g (13 oz) cans **chopped tomatoes**
600 ml (1 pint) **vegetable stock**
400 g (13 oz) can **borlotti beans**, drained
125 g (4 oz) **dried small pasta shapes**
**salt and black pepper**
grated **Parmesan cheese**, to serve

**For the basil oil**
25 g (1 oz) **basil leaves**
150 ml (¼ pint) **extra virgin olive oil**

**Heat** the oil in saucepan, add the onion, garlic and rosemary and cook over a low heat, stirring frequently, for 5 minutes until the onion is softened.

**Stir** in the tomatoes, stock, beans and salt and pepper. Bring to the boil, then reduce the heat, cover and simmer gently for 20 minutes. Add the pasta and simmer, covered, for a further 10 minutes until the pasta is al dente.

**Meanwhile**, make the basil oil. Plunge the basil leaves into a saucepan of boiling water, return to the boil and boil for 30 seconds. Drain the basil, refresh under cold water and dry thoroughly with kitchen paper. Transfer the oil and basil leaves to a blender and blend until really smooth.

**Ladle** the soup into bowls and spoon a little of the basil oil over each serving. Serve immediately, scattered with some grated Parmesan.

**For spiced tomato & Mexican bean soup**, replace the rosemary with thyme and the borlotti beans with a drained 400 g (13 oz) can of red kidney beans. Continue as above, omitting the pasta and adding 2 tablespoons chilli sauce to the soup. Serve the soup topped with soured cream.

# mushroom ramen

Serves **4**
Preparation time **10 minutes**
Cooking time **15 minutes**

300 g (10 oz) **dried ramen noodles**
1.5 litres (2½ pints) **vegetable stock**
75 ml (3 fl oz) **dark soy sauce**
3 tablespoons **mirin**
350 g (11½ oz) **mixed mushrooms**, trimmed
4 **spring onions**, trimmed and thinly sliced
300 g (10 oz) **silken tofu**, drained and diced

**Cook** the noodles according to the packet instructions. Drain well in a colander, refresh under cold water and set aside.

**Combine** the stock, soy sauce and mirin in a saucepan and bring to the boil, then reduce the heat and simmer gently for 5 minutes. Add the mushrooms and simmer gently for a further 5 minutes. Add the spring onions and tofu.

**Meanwhile**, boil a full kettle of water. Set the noodles, still in the colander, over a sink and pour over the boiling water. Divide the noodles between serving bowls and add the soup. Serve immediately.

**For vegetable ramen**, omit the mushrooms and replace with 125 g (4 oz) broccoli florets, 125 g (4 oz) sugar snap peas and 125 g (4 oz) trimmed asparagus, cut into short lengths. Simmer in the broth for 3 minutes and continue as in the recipe above. Ramen noodles are available from Japanese food stores and most health-food stores.

# saffron-scented vegetable tagine

Serves **4**
Preparation time **15 minutes**
Cooking time **50 minutes**

100 ml (3½ fl oz)
  **sunflower oil**
1 large **onion**, finely chopped
2 **garlic cloves**, crushed
2 teaspoons ground
  **coriander**
2 teaspoons ground **cumin**
2 teaspoons ground
  **cinnamon**
400 g (13 oz) can **chickpeas**,
  drained
400 g (13 oz) can **chopped
  tomatoes**
600 ml (1 pint) **vegetable
  stock**
¼ teaspoon **saffron threads**
1 large **aubergine**, trimmed
  and chopped
250 g (8 oz) **button
  mushrooms**, trimmed and
  halved if large
100 g (3½ oz) **dried figs**,
  chopped
2 tablespoons chopped **fresh
  coriander**
**salt and black pepper**

**Heat** 2 tablespoons of the oil in a frying pan, add the onion, garlic and spices and cook over a medium heat, stirring frequently, for 5 minutes until golden. Using a slotted spoon, transfer to a saucepan and add the chickpeas, tomatoes, stock and saffron. Season with salt and pepper.

**Heat** the remaining oil in the frying pan, add the aubergine and cook over a high heat, stirring frequently, for 5 minutes until browned. Add to the stew and bring to the boil, then reduce the heat, cover and simmer gently for 20 minutes.

**Stir** in the mushrooms and figs and simmer gently, uncovered, for a further 20 minutes. Stir in the fresh coriander and adjust the seasoning. Serve with steamed couscous.

**For winter vegetable & lentil tagine**, replace the aubergine with 2 sliced carrots and 2 cubed potatoes. Instead of the chickpeas use a drained 400 g (13 oz) can of green lentils. Follow the recipe above and stir in 100 g (3½ oz) dried apricots instead of the figs.

# goulash with chive dumplings

Serves **4**

Preparation time **30 minutes**

Cooking time **45 minutes**

4 tablespoons **olive oil**
8 **baby onions**, peeled
2 **garlic cloves**, crushed
1 **carrot**, chopped
1 large **celery stick**, sliced
500 g (1 lb) **potatoes**, cubed
1 teaspoon **caraway seeds**
1 teaspoon **smoked paprika**
400 g (13 oz) can **chopped tomatoes**
450 ml (¾ pint) **vegetable stock**
**salt and black pepper**

**For the chive dumplings**
75 g (3 oz) **self-raising flour**
½ teaspoon **salt**
50 g (2 oz) **vegetarian suet**
1 tablespoon chopped **chives**
4–5 tablespoons **water**

**Heat** the oil in a large saucepan, add the onions, garlic, carrot, celery, potatoes and caraway seeds and cook over a medium heat, stirring frequently, for 10 minutes. Add the paprika and cook, stirring, for 1 minute.

**Stir** in the tomatoes, stock and salt and pepper. Bring to the boil, then reduce the heat, cover and simmer gently for 20 minutes.

**Make** the dumplings. Sift the flour and salt into a bowl and stir in the suet, chives and pepper to taste. Working quickly and lightly, gradually mix in enough of the measurement water to form a soft dough. Divide into 8 equal pieces and roll into balls.

**Carefully** arrange the dumplings in the stew, leaving gaps between them, cover and simmer for 15 minutes until doubled in size and light and fluffy.

**For horseradish dumplings**, follow the method above, using 2 teaspoons grated fresh horseradish instead of the chopped chives. Continue with the recipe as above. These dumplings are especially good with beetroot: omit the tomatoes, increase the stock to 600 ml (1 pint) and add 275 g (9 oz) cooked beetroot.

# provençal vegetable stew

Serves **4**

Preparation time **15 minutes**

Cooking time **55 minutes**

4 tablespoons **extra virgin olive oil**, plus extra for drizzling

1 large **red onion**, sliced

4 **garlic cloves**, chopped

2 teaspoons **ground coriander**

1 tablespoon chopped **thyme**

1 **fennel bulb**, trimmed and sliced

1 **red pepper**, cored, deseeded and sliced

500 g (1 lb) **vine-ripened tomatoes**, diced

300 ml (½ pint) **vegetable stock**

125 g (4 oz) **Niçoise olives**

2 tablespoons chopped **parsley**

slices of **crusty bread**

**salt and black pepper**

**Heat** the oil in a large saucepan, add the onion, garlic, coriander and thyme and cook over a medium heat, stirring frequently, for 5 minutes until the onion is softened. Add the fennel and red pepper and cook, stirring frequently, for 10 minutes until softened.

**Stir** in the tomatoes, stock and salt and pepper. Bring to the boil, then reduce the heat, cover and simmer gently for 30 minutes. Stir in the olives and parsley and simmer, uncovered, for a further 10 minutes.

**Meanwhile,** heat a ridged griddle pan until hot. Add the bread slices and cook until toasted and charred on both sides. Drizzle liberally with oil.

**Serve** the stew hot with the toasted bread.

**For pasta with Provençal sauce**, cook 450 g (14½ oz) dried penne in a large saucepan of lightly salted boiling water for 10–12 minutes, or according to the packet instructions, until al dente. Drain well and top the pasta with the vegetable stew, used as a pasta sauce.

# fennel, pernod & orange casserole

Serves **4**

Preparation time **15 minutes**

Cooking time **about 50 minutes**

2 **fennel bulbs**, trimmed

4 tablespoons **extra virgin olive oil**

1 **onion**, chopped

2 **garlic cloves**, crushed

2 teaspoons chopped **rosemary**

**salt and black pepper**

100 ml (3½ fl oz) **Pernod**

400 g (13 oz) can **chopped tomatoes**

¼ teaspoon **saffron threads**

2 strips of **orange rind**

2 tablespoons chopped **fennel fronds**

**Chargrilled Polenta Triangles**, to serve (see page 170)

**Cut** the fennel lengthways into 5 mm (¼ inch) thick slices. Heat half the oil in a flameproof casserole, add the fennel slices, in batches, and cook over a medium heat for 3–4 minutes on each side until golden. Remove with a slotted spoon.

**Heat** the remaining oil in the casserole, add the onion, garlic, rosemary and salt and pepper and cook over a low heat, stirring frequently, for 5 minutes. Add the Pernod, bring to the boil and boil until reduced by half. Add the tomatoes, saffron and orange rind and stir well. Arrange the fennel slices over the top.

**Bring** the casserole to the boil, then cover with a tight-fitting lid and bake in a preheated oven, 180°C (350°F), Gas Mark 4, for 35 minutes until the fennel is tender. Stir in the fennel fronds and serve the casserole hot with some Chargrilled Polenta Triangles.

**For fennel gratin**, prepare the fennel casserole as in the recipe above and transfer to a gratin dish. Combine 125 g (4 oz) fresh white breadcrumbs, 4 tablespoons grated Parmesan and 2 tablespoons chopped parsley. Scatter over the top of the fennel mixture and bake, uncovered, for 35 minutes.

# home baked beans

Serves **4–6**
Preparation time **10 minutes**
Cooking time **about 2 hours**

2 x 400 g (13 oz) cans
**borlotti beans**, drained
1 **garlic clove**, crushed
1 **onion**, finely chopped
450 ml (¾ pint) **vegetable
stock**
300 ml (½ pint) **passata**
(sieved tomatoes)
2 tablespoons **molasses or
black treacle**
2 tablespoons **tomato purée**
2 tablespoons **soft dark
brown sugar**
1 tablespoon **Dijon mustard**
1 tablespoon **red wine
vinegar**
**salt and black pepper**

**Put** all the ingredients in a flameproof casserole with a little salt and pepper. Cover and bring slowly to the boil.

**Bake** in a preheated oven, 160°C (325°F), Gas Mark 3, for 1½ hours. Remove the lid and bake for a further 30 minutes until the sauce is syrupy. Serve with hot buttered toast.

**For home baked beans with jacket potatoes**, scrub 4 Desiree or King Edward potatoes, about 250 g (8 oz) each, then bake in a preheated oven, 200°C (400°F), Gas Mark 6, for about 1 hour until cooked through. Cut lengthways in half, season with salt and pepper and spoon over the beans. Grate over a little Cheddar before serving. The home baked beans are even better made a day ahead and heated through before serving.

# salads & sides

# tomato, avocado & peach salad

Serves **4**
Preparation time **15 minutes**,
  plus cooling
Cooking time **20 minutes**

4 **plum tomatoes**, sliced
1 **avocado**, peeled, stoned
  and sliced
250 g (8 oz) **buffalo
  mozzarella cheese**, sliced
1 ripe **peach**, stoned and
  diced
50 g (2 oz) pitted **black olives**
1 **red chilli**, deseeded and
  finely chopped
3 tablespoons **extra virgin
  olive oil**, plus extra for
  drizzling
juice of 1 **lime**
1 tablespoon chopped **fresh
  coriander**
**salt and black pepper**

**For the balsamic glaze**
600 ml (1 pint) **balsamic
  vinegar**

**First** make the balsamic glaze. Pour the vinegar into a
saucepan and bring to the boil. Reduce the heat and
simmer gently for 20 minutes, or until reduced to about
150 ml (¼ pint). Leave to cool completely.

**Arrange** the tomatoes, avocado and mozzarella on a
large platter. Combine the peach, olives, chilli, oil, lime
juice, coriander and salt and pepper in a bowl, stir well
and spoon over the salad.

**Drizzle** the salad with a little extra oil and the balsamic
glaze and serve.

**For classic Italian tricolore salad**, arrange 4 sliced
tomatoes, 1 sliced avocado, 250 g (8 oz) sliced
buffalo mozzarella and a few torn basil leaves on a
platter. Drizzle over some extra virgin olive oil and
a little white wine vinegar, and season with salt
and cracked black pepper.

# charred leek salad with hazelnuts

Serves **4**

Preparation time **10 minutes**

Cooking time **12–16 minutes**

500 g (1 lb) **baby leeks**

1–2 tablespoons
  **hazelnut oil**

dash of **lemon juice**

40 g (1½ oz) blanched
  **hazelnuts**

2 Little Gem or cos
  **lettuce hearts**

a few **mint sprigs**

15 g (½ oz) **pecorino cheese**

20 **black olives**, to garnish

**For the dressing**

4 tablespoons **hazelnut oil**

2 tablespoons **extra virgin
  olive oil**

2 teaspoons **sherry vinegar**

**salt and black pepper**

**Brush** the leeks with the hazelnut oil. Cook, in batches, on a preheated hot ridged griddle pan or under a preheated hot grill, turning frequently, for 6–8 minutes until evenly browned and cooked through. Toss with the lemon juice and season with salt and pepper. Leave to cool.

**Meanwhile**, heat a heavy-based frying pan until hot, add the hazelnuts and cook over a medium heat, stirring, for 3–4 minutes until browned. Leave to cool slightly and then roughly chop. Separate the lettuce leaves and pull the mint leaves from the sprigs.

**Arrange** the leeks in serving bowls or on plates and top with the lettuce leaves, mint and hazelnuts. Whisk all the dressing ingredients together in a small bowl, season with salt and pepper and pour over the salad. Shave the pecorino over the salad and serve garnished with the olives.

**For charred asparagus salad with pine nuts**, replace the leeks with the same quantity of trimmed asparagus. Brush with extra virgin olive oil rather than hazelnut oil, and cook and dress as in the recipe above. Toast pine nuts instead of hazelnuts, and use tarragon leaves in place of mint. For the dressing, use 4 tablespoons extra virgin olive oil, 2 tablespoons grapeseed oil, 2 teaspoons tarragon vinegar and the grated rind of 1 lemon, reserving a few thin strips of rind. Shave a little Parmesan over the salad and garnish with the reserved lemon rind strips.

# watermelon, fennel & feta salad

Serves **4**
Preparation time **10 minutes**
Cooking time **2 minutes**

350 g (11½ oz) fresh or frozen
    shelled **broad beans**
1 large **fennel bulb**
250 g (8 oz) **watermelon
    flesh,** diced
125 g (4 oz) **feta cheese**,
    crumbled
**salt and black pepper**

**For the dressing**
3 tablespoons **extra virgin
    olive oil**
1 tablespoon **lemon juice**
1 teaspoon **clear honey**
1 teaspoon **pomegranate
    syrup**

**Cook** the beans in a large saucepan of lightly salted boiling water for 2 minutes. Drain and immediately refresh under cold water. Pat dry with kitchen paper, then peel off and discard the tough outer skins. Put the beans in a bowl.

**Trim** the fennel bulb. Cut in half, then crossways into wafer-thin slices. Add to the beans with the watermelon and feta.

**Whisk** all the dressing ingredients together in a small bowl and season with salt and pepper. Pour over the salad, toss well and serve.

**For fennel, orange & parsley salad**, very thinly slice a large fennel bulb into a bowl and add ½ bunch of parsley, 2 tablespoons drained baby capers and 1 peeled and segmented orange. Add the juice of ½ lemon, 1 tablespoon orange juice and a good spoonful of extra virgin olive oil. Season with salt and pepper and mix well to combine.

# spiced couscous salad

Serves **4**

Preparation time **15 minutes**,
plus soaking

Cooking time **3 minutes**

200 ml (7 fl oz) **vegetable
stock**

200 ml (7 fl oz) **orange juice**

1 teaspoon ground
**cinnamon**

½ teaspoon ground
**coriander**

250 g (8 oz) **couscous**

75 g (3 oz) **raisins**

2 ripe **tomatoes**, chopped

¼ **preserved lemon**, chopped
(optional)

½ bunch of **parsley**, roughly
chopped

½ bunch of **mint**, roughly
chopped

1 **garlic clove**, crushed

4 tablespoons **extra virgin
olive oil**

**salt and black pepper**

**Combine** the stock, orange juice, spices and
½ teaspoon salt in a saucepan. Bring to the boil and
stir in the couscous. Remove from the heat, cover
and leave to soak for 10 minutes.

**Put** the raisins, tomatoes, preserved lemon, if using,
herbs, garlic and oil in a large bowl and toss well. Stir
in the soaked couscous and season with salt and
pepper. Serve warm or leave to cool and serve at
room temperature.

**For couscous tabbouleh**, follow the recipe above
for the first step, then stir in 4 chopped ripe tomatoes,
½ diced cucumber, 1 small diced red onion, ½ bunch
each of chopped parsley and mint, 4 tablespoons
extra virgin olive oil, the juice of 1 lemon and salt and
pepper to taste. Toss well and taste, adding more
lemon juice, if you like.

# middle eastern bread salad

Serves **4–6**

Preparation time **10 minutes**, plus cooling

2 **flatbreads or flour tortillas**
1 large **green pepper**, cored, deseeded and diced
1 **Lebanese cucumber**, diced
250 g (8 oz) **cherry tomatoes**, halved
½ **red onion**, finely chopped
2 tablespoons chopped **mint**
2 tablespoons chopped **parsley**
2 tablespoons chopped **fresh coriander**
3 tablespoons **extra virgin olive oil**
juice of 1 **lemon**
**salt and black pepper**

**Cook** the flatbreads on a preheated ridged griddle pan or under a preheated hot grill for 2–3 minutes until toasted and charred. Leave to cool, then tear into bite-sized pieces.

**Put** the green pepper, cucumber, tomatoes, onion and herbs in a bowl, add the oil, lemon juice and salt and pepper and stir well. Add the bread and stir again. Serve immediately.

**For tomato & bread salad**, chop 750 g (1½ lb) ripe tomatoes into a bowl and add 4 slices of diced day-old bread, 1 bunch of basil leaves, 125 g (4 oz) pitted black olives, 75 ml (3 fl oz) extra virgin olive oil, 1 tablespoon balsamic vinegar and salt and pepper. Toss well and serve.

# new potato, basil & pine nut salad

Serves **4–6**
Preparation time **5 minutes**,
  plus cooling
Cooking time **15 minutes**

1 kg (2 lb) **new potatoes**,
  scrubbed
4 tablespoons **extra virgin
  olive oil**
1½ tablespoons **white wine
  vinegar**
50 g (2 oz) **pine nuts**,
  toasted
½ bunch of **basil leaves**
**salt and black pepper**

**Put** the potatoes in a large saucepan of lightly salted water and bring to the boil. Cook for 12–15 minutes until tender. Drain well and transfer to a large bowl. Cut any large potatoes in half.

**Whisk** the oil, vinegar and a little salt and pepper together in a small bowl. Add half to the potatoes, stir well and leave to cool completely.

**Add** the pine nuts, the remaining dressing and basil, stir well and serve.

**For traditional potato salad**, cook 1 kg (2 lb) new potatoes as above, drain and leave to cool. Combine 150 ml (¼ pint) good-quality mayonnaise with 1 bunch of finely chopped spring onions, 2 tablespoons chopped fresh chives, a squeeze of lemon juice and salt and pepper. Toss with the potatoes.

# spinach & gorgonzola salad

Serves **4**

Preparation time **5 minutes**,
plus cooling

Cooking time **3 minutes**

1 tablespoon **clear honey**

125 g (4 oz) **walnut halves**

250 g (8 oz) **French beans**,
trimmed

200 g (7 oz) **baby spinach
leaves**

150 g (5 oz) **Gorgonzola
cheese**, crumbled

**For the dressing**

4 tablespoons **walnut oil**

2 tablespoons **extra virgin
olive oil**

1–2 tablespoons **sherry
vinegar**

**salt and black pepper**

**Heat** the honey in a small frying pan, add the walnuts and stir-fry over a medium heat for 2–3 minutes until the nuts are glazed. Tip on to a plate and leave to cool.

**Meanwhile**, cook the beans in a saucepan of lightly salted boiling water for 3 minutes. Drain, refresh under cold water and shake dry. Put in a large bowl with the spinach leaves.

**Whisk** all the dressing ingredients together in a small bowl and season with salt and pepper. Pour over the salad and toss well. Arrange the salad in serving bowls, scatter over the Gorgonzola and glazed walnuts and serve immediately.

**For watercress, almond & Stilton salad**, replace the spinach with an equal weight of watercress. Dress with 50 g (2 oz) toasted flaked almonds, 200 g (7 oz) crumbled Stilton instead of the Gorgonzola, and a drizzle of olive oil.

# greek country salad with haloumi

Serves **4**
Preparation time **10 minutes**
Cooking time **2 minutes**

4 **vine-ripened tomatoes**,
  roughly chopped
½ **onion**, sliced
1 **Lebanese cucumber**,
  thickly sliced
100 g (3½ oz) pitted **black
  Kalamata olives**
1 small **cos lettuce**
250 g (8 oz) **haloumi cheese**,
  sliced

**For the dressing**
4 tablespoons **extra virgin
  olive oil**
1½ tablespoons **red wine
  vinegar**
1 teaspoon **dried oregano**
**salt and black pepper**

**Put** the tomatoes, onion, cucumber and olives in a
bowl. Tear the lettuce into pieces and add to the salad.
Toss well and arrange on a large platter.

**Whisk** all the dressing ingredients together in a small
bowl and season with salt and pepper. Drizzle a little
over the salad.

**Heat** a heavy-based frying pan until hot, add the
haloumi slices and cook for 1 minute on each side until
charred and softened. Arrange on top of the salad,
drizzle over the remaining dressing and serve
immediately.

**For Greek salad with chunky croûtons**, replace the
haloumi with 200 g (7 oz) crumbled feta cheese. To
make the croûtons, cut thick slices of close-textured
country bread, then cut these into large chunks. Heat
a little olive oil in a frying pan and fry the bread,
turning occasionally, until crisp and golden. Add extra
olive oil as needed. Cool, then toss into the salad and
serve immediately.

# fig, bean & toasted pecan salad

Serves **4**

Preparation time **5 minutes**,
   plus cooling

Cooking time **5–6 minutes**

100 g (3½ oz) **pecan nuts**

200 g (7 oz) **French beans**,
   trimmed

4 ripe fresh **figs**, cut into
   quarters

100 g (3½ oz) **rocket leaves**

small handful of **mint leaves**

50 g (2 oz) **Parmesan or
   pecorino cheese**

**For the dressing**

3 tablespoons **walnut oil**

2 teaspoons **sherry vinegar**

1 teaspoon **vincotto**

**salt and black pepper**

**Heat** a heavy-based frying pan until hot, add the
pecan nuts and cook over a medium heat, stirring,
for 3–4 minutes until browned. Leave to cool.

**Cook** the beans in a saucepan of lightly salted boiling
water for 2 minutes. Drain, refresh under cold water
and pat dry with kitchen paper. Put the beans in a bowl
with the figs, pecan nuts, rocket and mint.

**Whisk** all the dressing ingredients together in a
small bowl and season with salt and paper. Pour
over the salad and toss well. Shave over the Parmesan
or pecorino.

**For mixed bean salad**, combine 200 g (7 oz) cooked
trimmed French beans with 2 x 400 g (13 oz) cans
drained mixed beans, 4 finely chopped spring onions,
1 crushed garlic clove and 4 tablespoons chopped
mixed herbs, then dress with 4 tablespoons extra
virgin olive oil, juice of ½ lemon, a pinch of caster
sugar and salt and pepper. If you can't find vincotto
(see page 13), use balsamic vinegar as an alternative.

# thai vegetable salad

Serves **4**

Preparation time **10 minutes**, plus cooling

Cooking time **2 minutes**

250 g (8 oz) **cherry tomatoes**, quartered

1 **Lebanese cucumber**, thinly sliced

1 **green papaya or green mango**

1 large **red chilli**, deseeded and thinly sliced

150 g (5 oz) **bean sprouts**

4 **spring onions**, trimmed and thinly sliced

small handful of **Thai basil leaves**

small handful of **mint leaves**

small handful of **fresh coriander leaves**

4 tablespoons **unsalted peanuts**, roughly chopped

**For the chilli dressing**

2 tablespoons **Chilli Jam** (see page 44)

2 tablespoons **light soy sauce**

2 tablespoons **lime juice**

4 teaspoons grated **palm sugar**

**First** make the dressing. Put all the ingredients in a small saucepan and warm over a low heat, stirring, until the sugar has dissolved. Leave to cool.

**Put** the tomatoes, cucumber, papaya or mango, chilli, bean sprouts, spring onions and herbs in a bowl. Add the dressing and toss well. Transfer to a platter. Sprinkle over the peanuts and serve immediately.

**For Thai salad wraps,** serve the salad with large iceberg lettuce leaves. Spoon a little salad on to the leaves, roll up and dip into the chilli dressing. To cool the chilli heat, make a dressing of soy sauce, lime juice and omit the palm sugar. Omit the chilli jam but add 2 tablespoons warmed lime marmalade instead.

# roast vegetables & parsley pesto

Serves **4**

Preparation time **15 minutes**

Cooking time **50 minutes–
  1 hour**

4 small **potatoes**, scrubbed

1 **red onion**

2 **carrots**

2 **parsnips**

8 **garlic cloves**, unpeeled

4 **thyme sprigs**

2 tablespoons **extra virgin
  olive oil**

**For the parsley pesto**

75 g (3 oz) blanched **almonds**

large bunch of **flat leaf
  parsley**

2 **garlic cloves**, chopped

150 ml (¼ pint) **extra virgin
  olive oil**

2 tablespoons grated
  **Parmesan cheese**

**salt and black pepper**

**Cut** the potatoes and onion into wedges and the carrots and parsnips into quarters. Put in a large roasting tin to fit in a single layer. Add the garlic cloves, thyme sprigs, oil and salt and pepper and stir well until evenly coated. Roast in a preheated oven, 220°C (425°F), Gas Mark 7, for 50 minutes–1 hour until browned and tender, stirring halfway through.

**Meanwhile**, make the pesto. Heat a heavy-based frying pan until hot, add the almonds and cook over a medium heat, stirring, for 3–4 minutes until browned. Transfer to a bowl and leave to cool.

**Put** the almonds in a mortar or food processor, add the parsley, garlic and salt and pepper and grind with a pestle or process to form a coarse paste. Transfer to a bowl, stir in the oil and Parmesan and adjust the seasoning.

**Serve** the roast vegetables hot with the pesto.

**For pasta with parsley pesto**, cook 450 g (14½ oz) dried pasta in a large saucepan of lightly salted boiling water according to the packet instructions, until al dente. Meanwhile, make the pesto. Drain the pasta, reserving 4 tablespoons of the cooking water. Return the pasta and the reserved pasta cooking water to the pan. Add the pesto, toss well and serve. The pasta can be served as a substantial base for the roast vegetables.

# spiced braised new potatoes

Serves **4–6**
Preparation time **15 minutes**
Cooking time **45 minutes**

50 g (2 oz) **butter**
1 small **onion**, finely chopped
1 **garlic clove**, crushed
1 teaspoon grated **fresh root ginger**
1 teaspoon ground **coriander**
½ teaspoon ground **turmeric**
½ teaspoon ground **cumin**
1 kg (2 lb) small **waxy potatoes**, scrubbed
300 ml (½ pint) **vegetable stock**
2 ripe **tomatoes**, diced
chopped **fresh coriander**, to garnish
**salt and black pepper**

**Melt** the butter in a saucepan, add the onion, garlic, ginger and spices and cook over a low heat, stirring frequently, for 5 minutes. Add the potatoes and salt and pepper, stir well and then add the stock and tomatoes to the pan.

**Bring** to the boil, then reduce the heat, cover and simmer gently for 20 minutes.

**Remove** the lid and simmer, uncovered, for a further 15–20 minutes until the liquid is reduced and thickened to a glaze. Serve hot, garnished with some chopped fresh coriander.

**For roasted new potatoes with garlic & rosemary**, put 1 kg (2 lb) scrubbed small waxy potatoes into a roasting tin with 12 whole unpeeled garlic cloves, 2 tablespoons chopped rosemary, 2 tablespoons olive oil and salt and pepper. Stir well and roast in a preheated oven, 200°C (400°F), Gas Mark 6, for 40–45 minutes until tender.

# vegetable tempura

Serves **4**
Preparation time **20 minutes**
Cooking time **about 20 minutes**

125 g (4 oz) **broccoli florets**
124 g (4 oz) **red pepper slices**
124 g (4 oz) **pumpkin slices**
125 g (4 oz) **trimmed green beans**
125 g (4 oz) **courgette slices**
**vegetable oil**, for deep-frying

For the dipping sauce
250 ml (8 fl oz) **vegetable stock**
1 tablespoon **wakame seaweed** (see page 13)
3 tablespoons **mirin**
3 tablespoons **dark soy sauce**

For the tempura batter
1 **egg yolk**
250 ml (8 fl oz) **cold water**
150 g (5 oz) **plain flour**

**First** make the dipping sauce. Put all the ingredients in a saucepan and heat over a low heat without boiling for 10 minutes. Keep warm.

**Meanwhile**, heat 5 cm (2 inches) vegetable oil in a wok or deep, heavy-based saucepan until it reaches 180–190°C (350–375°F), or until a cube of bread browns in 30 seconds.

**Quickly** whisk all the batter ingredients together in a bowl. Dip the vegetables in the batter, a few at a time, add to the hot oil and deep-fry for 2–3 minutes until crisp and lightly coloured. Remove with a slotted spoon and drain on kitchen paper. Keep warm in a moderate oven while cooking the remainder.

**Serve** the vegetable tempura with the dipping sauce.

**For ponzu dipping sauce**, combine 2 tablespoons dark soy sauce, 4 tablespoons rice wine vinegar and 1 tablespoon lemon juice, and serve with the vegetable tempura.

# baked sweet potatoes

Serves **4**
Preparation time **5 minutes**
Cooking time **45–50 minutes**

4 **sweet potatoes**, about
   250 g (8 oz) each, scrubbed
200 g (7 oz) **soured cream**
2 **spring onions**, trimmed and
   finely chopped
1 tablespoon chopped **chives**
50 g (2 oz) **butter**
**salt and black pepper**

**Put** the potatoes in a roasting tin and roast in a preheated oven, 220°C (425°F), Gas Mark 7, for 45–50 minutes until cooked through.

**Meanwhile**, combine the soured cream, spring onions, chives and salt and pepper in a bowl.

**Cut** the baked potatoes in half lengthways, top with the butter and spoon over the soured cream mixture. Serve immediately.

**For crispy sweet potato skins**, allow the baked sweet potatoes to cool, cut into wedges and cut out some of the soft potato, leaving a good lining inside the skin. Deep fry in hot oil for 4–5 minutes until crisp. Serve with soured cream and chopped chives to dip.

# indian-spiced pumpkin wedges

Serves **4**

Preparation time **15 minutes**, plus cooling

Cooking time **15–20 minutes**

1 kg (2 lb) **pumpkin or butternut squash**

1 teaspoon **cumin seeds**

1 teaspoon **coriander seeds**

2 **cardamom pods**

3 tablespoons **sunflower oil**

1 teaspoon **caster sugar or mango chutney**

**For the coconut pesto**

25 g (1 oz) **fresh coriander leaves**

1 **garlic clove**, crushed

1 **green chilli**, deseeded and chopped

pinch of **caster sugar**

1 tablespoon **pistachio nuts**, roughly chopped

6 tablespoons **coconut cream**

1 tablespoon **lime juice**

**salt and black pepper**

**Cut** the pumpkin or squash into thin wedges about 1 cm (½ inch) thick, discarding the seeds and fibres, and put in a large dish.

**Heat** a heavy-based frying pan until hot, add the whole spices and cook over a medium heat, stirring, until browned. Leave to cool, then grind to a powder in a spice grinder or in a mortar with a pestle. Mix the ground spices with the oil and sugar or mango chutney in a small bowl, then add to the pumpkin wedges and toss well to coat.

**Cook** the pumpkin or squash wedges under a preheated hot grill, or over a preheated hot gas barbecue or the hot coals of a charcoal barbecue, for 6–8 minutes on each side until charred and tender.

**Meanwhile**, make the pesto. Put the coriander leaves, garlic, chilli, sugar and pistachio nuts in a food processor and process until fairly finely ground and blended. Season with salt and pepper. Add the coconut cream and lime juice and process again. Transfer to a serving bowl.

**Serve** the wedges hot with the coconut pesto.

**For Indian-spiced sweet potato wedges**, cook 4 scrubbed sweet potatoes, 250 g (8 oz) each, in a large saucepan of simmering water for 15 minutes, or until just tender, then drain. When cool enough to handle, slice into large wedges. Toss with the spice and oil mixture and grill or barbecue, as above, for about 6 minutes, turning frequently, until browned. Serve hot with the coconut pesto.

# chargrilled polenta triangles

Serves **8**

Preparation time **5 minutes**, plus cooling

Cooking time **15–20 minutes**

**spray oil**, for oiling

1 litre (1¾ pints) **water**

2 teaspoons **salt**

175 g (6 oz) **instant polenta**

2 **garlic cloves**, crushed

50 g (2 oz) **butter**

50 g (2 oz) **Parmesan cheese**, freshly grated, plus extra to serve

**olive oil**, for brushing

chopped **fresh parsley**, to garnish

**black pepper**

**Lightly** oil a 23 x 30 cm (9 x 12 inch) baking tin with spray oil. Bring the measurement water to the boil in a heavy-based saucepan, add the salt and then gradually whisk in the polenta in a steady stream. Cook over a low heat, stirring constantly with a wooden spoon, for 5 minutes until the grains have swelled and thickened.

**Remove** from the heat and immediately beat in the garlic, butter, Parmesan and pepper until smooth. Pour the mixture into the prepared tin and leave to cool.

**Turn** the polenta out on to a chopping board and cut into large squares, then diagonally in half into triangles. Brush the triangles with a little oil.

**Heat** a ridged griddle pan until hot. Add the polenta triangles, in batches, and cook over a medium-high heat for 2–3 minutes on each side until charred and heated through. Serve immediately, garnished with grated Parmesan and chopped parsley.

**For soft polenta with sage butter**, melt 125 g (4 oz) butter in a small saucepan. Add 1 tablespoon chopped sage and a pinch of cayenne pepper to the butter and cook over a medium-high heat, stirring, for 2–3 minutes until the sage is crisp and the butter turns golden brown. Keep warm. Follow the above recipe to the end of the first stage. Remove the cooked polenta from the heat and stir in 50 g (2 oz) grated Parmesan. Pour into bowls and serve drizzled with the sage butter.

# breads &
# baking

# fig, goats' cheese & tapenade tart

Serves **4**

Preparation time **10 minutes**

Cooking time **20–25 minutes**

350 g (11½ oz) **puff pastry**, defrosted if frozen

**plain flour**, for dusting

1 **egg**, beaten

3 tablespoons ready-made **olive tapenade**

3 fresh ripe **figs**, quartered

100 g (3½ oz) **cherry tomatoes**, halved

100 g (3½ oz) **soft goats' cheese**, crumbled

2 teaspoons chopped **thyme**

2 tablespoons freshly grated **Parmesan cheese**

**Rocket Salad**, to serve (see page 56) (optional)

**Roll** the pastry out on a lightly floured work surface until 2 mm (¼ inch) thick to form a rectangle 20 x 30 cm (8 x 12 inches), trimming the edges. Prick the pastry with a fork and score a border 2.5 cm (1 inch) in from the edges. Transfer to a baking sheet. Brush the pastry with a little beaten egg and bake in a preheated oven, 200°C (400°F), Gas Mark 6, for 12–15 minutes.

**Remove** the pastry from the oven and carefully press down the centre to flatten slightly. Spread the centre with the tapenade and then arrange the figs, tomatoes, goats' cheese, thyme and Parmesan over the top.

**Return** the tart to the oven and bake for a further 5–10 minutes until the pastry is golden, the cheese is melted and the figs are cooked. Brown the top under a preheated hot grill, if liked, making sure that the pastry edges don't burn (you can cover them with foil). Serve warm with a rocket salad, if wished.

**For grilled vegetable & goats' cheese tart**, thinly slice 1 courgette and 1 aubergine, core, deseed and quarter 1 red pepper and cut 1 red onion into thin wedges. Brush the vegetables with olive oil and cook under a preheated hot grill for 3–4 minutes on each side until tender. Use the grilled vegetables in place of the figs and tomatoes, and continue with the recipe as above.

# mixed mushroom tart

Serves **6**
Preparation time **45 minutes**,
   plus chilling and cooling
Cooking time **50–55 minutes**

50 g (2 oz) **butter**
6 **shallots**, finely chopped
2 **garlic cloves**, crushed
2 teaspoons chopped **thyme**
350 g (11½ oz) mixed
   **mushrooms**, such as
   shiitake, oyster, brown and
   field, trimmed and sliced
300 ml (½ pint) **soured cream**
3 **eggs**, lightly beaten
25 g (1 oz) **Parmesan
   cheese**, freshly grated
**salt and black pepper**
**rocket leaves**, to serve

**For the pastry**
200 g (7 oz) **plain flour**, plus
   extra for dusting
½ teaspoon **salt**
125 g (4 oz) chilled **unsalted
   butter**, diced
1 **egg yolk**
2 tablespoons **cold water**

**First** make the pastry. Sift the flour and salt into a bowl. Add the butter and rub in with the fingertips until the mixture resembles fine breadcrumbs. Add the egg yolk and measurement water and bring the mixture together. Wrap in clingfilm and chill for 30 minutes.

**Roll** the pastry out on a lightly floured work surface. Use to line a 25 cm (10 inch) fluted flan tin. Prick the base with a fork and chill for 30 minutes. Line the pastry with nonstick baking paper and baking beans and bake in a preheated oven, 200°C (400°F), Gas Mark 6, for 15 minutes. Remove the paper and beans and bake for a further 15 minutes. Leave to cool.

**Meanwhile**, melt the butter in a frying pan, add the shallots, garlic and thyme and cook over a low heat, stirring frequently, for 5 minutes. Increase the heat, add the mushrooms and salt and pepper and cook, stirring, for 4–5 minutes until browned. Leave to cool. Scatter over the tart case. Beat the soured cream, eggs, Parmesan and salt and pepper together and pour over the top. Bake for 20–25 minutes until golden and just set. Serve warm with some rocket leaves.

**For spinach & feta tart**, replace the mushrooms with 500 g (1 lb) frozen leaf spinach, defrosted and squeezed dry. Add to the cooked shallot mixture and spread over the tart case. Add the soured cream mixture and scatter over 125 g (4 oz) crumbled feta cheese. Continue as above.

# tomato & feta tart

Serves **4**
Preparation time **15 minutes**
Cooking time **20 minutes**

350 g (11½ oz) **puff pastry**,
   defrosted if frozen
**plain flour**, for dusting
3 tablespoons **Pesto** (see
   page 86)
250 g (8 oz) **baby plum
   tomatoes,** halved
100 g (3½ oz) **feta cheese**,
   crumbled
4 tablespoons freshly grated
   **Parmesan cheese**
handful of **basil leaves**
**salt and black pepper**

**Roll** the pastry out on a lightly floured work surface to
form a rectangle 25 x 35 cm (10 x 14 inches). Using a
sharp knife, score a 2.5 cm (1 inch) border around the
edges. Transfer to a baking sheet and spread the pesto
over the pastry.

**Arrange** the tomatoes and feta over the top and
scatter over the Parmesan. Season with salt and
pepper. Bake in a preheated oven, 220°C (425°F),
Gas Mark 7, for 20 minutes until the pastry is puffed
and golden. Remove from the oven and scatter over
the basil leaves.

**For individual tartlets**, roll the pastry out to a
rectangle 25 x 37.5 cm (10 x 15 inches). Cut in
half lengthways and then across into 3, to make
6 x 12.5 cm (5 inch) squares. Divide the pesto and
toppings equally between the squares and bake for
15 minutes or until puffed up and golden.

# mixed seed soda bread

Makes **1 small loaf**
Preparation time **10 minutes**
Cooking time **40–45 minutes**

**spray oil**, for oiling
350 g (11½ oz) **wholemeal plain flour**, plus extra for dusting and sprinkling
50 g (2 oz) **sunflower seeds**
2 tablespoons **poppy seeds**
1 teaspoon **bicarbonate of soda**
1 teaspoon **salt**
1 teaspoon **caster sugar**
300 ml (½ pint) **buttermilk**

**Lightly** oil a baking sheet with spray oil. Mix the flour, sunflower seeds, poppy seeds, bicarbonate of soda, salt and sugar together in a bowl. Make a well in the centre, add the buttermilk and gradually work into the flour mixture to form a soft dough.

**Turn** the dough out on a lightly floured work surface and knead for 5 minutes. Shape into a flattish round. Transfer to the prepared baking sheet. Using a sharp knife, cut a cross in the top of the bread. Sprinkle a little extra flour over the surface.

**Bake** in a preheated oven, 230°C (450°F), Gas Mark 8, for 15 minutes, then reduce the temperature to 200°C (400°F), Gas Mark 6, and bake for a further 25–30 minutes until risen and the loaf sounds hollow when tapped underneath. Leave to cool completely on a wire rack.

**For pinhead oatmeal soda bread**, follow the above recipe, replacing the sunflower seeds with an equal quantity of pinhead oatmeal. Omit the poppy seeds and continue as above.

# chilli & sweetcorn cornbread

Serves **8–12**
Preparation time **10 minutes**
Cooking time **30–40 minutes**

**spray oil**, for oiling
75 g (3 oz) **plain flour**
1 tablespoon **baking powder**
200 g (7 oz) **medium cornmeal**
1 teaspoon **salt**
3 **eggs**, beaten
300 ml (½ pint) **natural yogurt**
4 tablespoons **sunflower oil**
200 g (7 oz) can **sweetcorn**, drained
1 large **red chilli**, deseeded and chopped

**Lightly** oil a 1 kg (2 lb) loaf tin with spray oil and line the base with nonstick baking paper.

**Sift** the flour and baking powder into a bowl and stir in the cornmeal and salt. Make a well in the centre. Mix the eggs, yogurt and oil together in a separate bowl. Add to the well and gradually beat into the flour mixture to make a smooth batter. Stir in the sweetcorn and chilli.

**Pour** the mixture into the prepared tin. Bake in a preheated oven, 200°C (400°F), Gas Mark 6, for 30–40 minutes. Leave to cool in the tin for 5 minutes, then turn out and leave to cool completely on a wire rack.

**For chilli & sweetcorn muffins**, line a 12-hole muffin tin with paper muffin cases. Divide the mixture among the prepared cases. Bake at 200°C (400°F), Gas Mark 6, for 20–25 minutes until risen and golden. Transfer to a wire rack and leave to cool.

# herb & cheese damper

Serves **8**

Preparation time **10 minutes**

Cooking time **30 minutes**

**spray oil**, for oiling

500 g (1 lb) **self-raising flour**, plus extra for dusting

½ teaspoon **salt**

15 g (½ oz) chilled **butter**, diced

50 g (2 oz) **Cheddar cheese**, grated

2 teaspoons chopped **rosemary**

150 ml (¼ pint) **milk**

150 ml (¼ pint) **water**

**Lightly** oil a baking sheet with spray oil. Sift the flour and salt into a bowl. Add the butter and rub in with the fingertips until the mixture resembles fine breadcrumbs. Stir in the Cheddar and rosemary. Make a well in the centre, add the milk and measurement water and gradually work into the flour mixture to form a soft dough.

**Turn** the dough out on a lightly floured work surface and knead gently into a smooth ball. Transfer the dough to the prepared baking sheet and flatten slightly to form an 18 cm (7 inch) round. Using a sharp knife, score the surface into 8 wedges. Bake in a preheated oven, 200°C (400°F), Gas Mark 6, for about 30 minutes until risen and the loaf sounds hollow when tapped underneath. Transfer to a wire rack and leave to cool completely.

**For individual rolls**, divide the dough into 8 pieces. Shape each piece into a ball and flatten slightly into a round. Brush each one with a little milk and scatter over a little extra grated Cheddar. Bake at 200°C (400°F), Gas Mark 6, for 18–20 minutes until cooked.

# aubergine & goats' cheese gratin

Serves **6**

Preparation time **10 minutes**

Cooking time **1 hour 10 minutes**

**spray oil**, for oiling

2 x 400 g (13 oz) cans **chopped tomatoes**

2 large **garlic cloves**, crushed

4 tablespoons **extra virgin olive oil**

1 teaspoon **caster sugar**

2 tablespoon chopped **basil**

2 **aubergines**

250 g (8 oz) **soft goats' cheese**, sliced or crumbled

50 g (2 oz) **Parmesan cheese**, freshly grated

**salt and black pepper**

**Lightly** oil a 1.5 litre (2½ pint) baking dish with spray oil. Put the tomatoes, garlic, half the oil, sugar, basil and salt and pepper in a saucepan and bring to the boil. Reduce the heat and simmer for 30 minutes until reduced and thickened.

**Cut** each aubergine lengthways into 6 thin slices. Season the remaining oil with salt and pepper, then brush the aubergine slices with the seasoned oil. Cook under a preheated hot grill for 3–4 minutes on each side until charred and tender.

**Arrange** one-third of the aubergine slices, overlapping them slightly, in the base of the prepared dish. Add one-third of the tomato sauce and one-third of the goats' cheese and Parmesan. Repeat these layers, finishing with the 2 cheeses. Bake in a preheated oven, 200°C (400°F), Gas Mark 6, for 30 minutes until bubbling and golden.

**For aubergine lasagne**, follow the above recipe to the end of the second stage, then set the aubergines and tomato sauce aside. Make 1 quantity Cheese Sauce (see page 90). Layer the aubergines, tomato sauce and cheese sauce in a 2 litre (3½ pint) baking dish, scatter 4 tablespoons grated Parmesan over the top and bake as above for 35–40 minutes until bubbling and golden.

# potato gratin with pine nut crust

Serves **6**

Preparation time **15 minutes**

Cooking time **1 1/2 hours**

**spray oil**, for oiling

1 kg (2 lb) small waxy
  **potatoes**

freshly grated **nutmeg**, to
  taste

25 g (1 oz) **butter**, diced

200 ml (7 fl oz) **milk**

200 ml (7 fl oz) **double cream**

**salt and black pepper**

**For the pine nut crust**

50 g (2 oz) fresh **wholemeal
  breadcrumbs**

50 g (2 oz) **pine nuts**

25 g (1 oz) **Parmesan
  cheese**, freshly grated

1 tablespoon chopped
  **parsley**

**Lightly** oil a 1 litre (1¾ pint) baking dish with spray oil.
Peel the potatoes, then cut into wafer-thin slices.
Arrange the slices, in overlapping layers, in the
prepared dish, seasoning each layer with nutmeg, salt
and pepper and adding small knobs of butter.

**Mix** the milk and cream together, pour over the
potatoes and cover the dish with foil. Bake in a
preheated oven, 190°C (375°F), Gas Mark 5, for
1 hour until the potatoes are almost tender.

**Meanwhile**, combine the breadcrumbs, pine nuts,
Parmesan and parsley in a bowl.

**Remove** the foil from the gratin and scatter the
breadcrumb mixture over to form a crust. Bake for
a further 25–30 minutes until the topping is crisp
and golden.

**For potato & parsnip gratin**, thinly slice 500 g (1 lb)
small waxy potatoes and 500 g (1 lb) parsnips and
arrange in alternate layers in a 1 litre (1¾ pint) baking
dish lightly oiled with spray oil. Continue as in the
recipe above.

# four cheese pizza

Makes **2**
Preparation time **20 minutes**,
  plus rising
Cooking time **20–30 minutes**

125 g (4 oz) **mozzarella cheese**, sliced
50 g (2 oz) **taleggio or fontina cheese**, diced
50 g (2 oz) **Gorgonzola cheese**, crumbled
4 tablespoons freshly grated **Parmesan cheese**
**rocket leaves**, to serve

**For the pizza dough**
250 g (8 oz) **white bread flour**, plus extra for dusting
1 teaspoon **fast-action dried yeast**
1 teaspoon **sea salt**
pinch of **caster sugar**
150 ml (¼ pint) **warm water**
1 tablespoon **extra virgin olive oil**
**spray oil**, for oiling

**First** make the pizza dough. Sift the flour into a bowl and stir in the yeast, salt and sugar. Make a well in the centre, add the measurement water and oil and gradually work into the flour mixture to form a soft dough.

**Lightly** oil a bowl with spray oil. Turn the dough out on a lightly floured work surface. Knead for 10 minutes until smooth and elastic. Put in the prepared bowl, cover and leave to rise in a warm place for 1 hour until doubled in size.

**Put** a heavy-based baking sheet on the middle shelf of a preheated oven, 230°C (450°F), Gas Mark 8, and heat for 5 minutes. Knock the air out of the dough. Divide in half. Roll one half out to a 25 cm (10 inch) round. Transfer to the heated baking sheet and scatter over half the cheeses. Bake for 10–15 minutes until the base is crisp and golden. Serve immediately, topped with rocket leaves. Repeat to make the second pizza.

**For cherry tomato & cheese pizza**, top each pizza base with 125 g (4 oz) halved cherry tomatoes, 125 g (4 oz) sliced mozzarella, 50 g (2 oz) pitted black olives and a few basil leaves. Bake as above. Cook the pizzas one at a time for the best results. To serve 4, simply double the quantities.

# roasted squash & sage pizza

Makes **2**

Preparation time **20 minutes**, plus rising

Cooking time **45–55 minutes**

**spray oil**, for oiling

1 quantity **Pizza Dough** (see page 190)

**white bread flour**, for dusting

500 g (1 lb) **butternut squash**, peeled

1 **onion**, sliced

2 tablespoons **extra virgin olive oil**

2 **garlic cloves**, finely chopped

pinch of **dried chilli flakes**

1 tablespoon chopped **sage**

250 g (8 oz) **mozzarella cheese**, sliced

4 tablespoons freshly grated **Parmesan cheese**

**salt and black pepper**

**Lightly** oil a bowl with spray oil. Turn the dough out on a lightly floured work surface. Knead for 10 minutes until smooth and elastic. Put in the prepared bowl, cover and leave to rise in a warm place for 1 hour until doubled in size.

**Meanwhile,** cut the squash in half and scoop out and discard the seeds and fibres. Cut into 2.5 cm (1 inch) dice. Put in a roasting tin, add the onion, half the oil, the garlic, chilli flakes, sage and salt and pepper and toss well. Roast in a preheated oven, 230°C (450°F), Gas Mark 8, for 25 minutes until tender, stirring halfway through.

**Put** a heavy-based baking sheet on the middle shelf of the oven and heat for 5 minutes. Knock the air out of the dough. Divide in half. Roll one half out to a 25 cm (10 inch) round. Transfer to the heated baking sheet. Top with half the squash mixture and half the cheeses. Bake for 10–15 minutes until the base is crisp and golden. Serve immediately. Repeat to make the second pizza.

**For roasted squash & sage calzone**, roll the entire dough out to form a large round 40 cm (16 inches) across. Arrange the squash mixture on one half and top with the cheeses. Dampen the edges with water, fold the remaining dough over the filling and press the edges together to seal. Bake on a baking sheet at the same temperature as above for 25–30 minutes until puffed and golden.

# asparagus & taleggio pizza

Makes **2**
Preparation time **15 minutes**,
  plus rising
Cooking time **20–30 minutes**

**spray oil**, for oiling
1 quantity **Pizza Dough** (see
  page 190)
**white bread flour**, for dusting
5 tablespoons **passata**
  (sieved tomatoes)
1 tablespoon ready-made **red
  pesto**
pinch of **salt**
250 g (8 oz) **taleggio cheese**,
  sliced
175 g (6 oz) **slim asparagus**,
  trimmed
2 tablespoons **olive oil**
**black pepper**

**Lightly** oil a bowl with spray oil. Turn the dough out on a lightly floured work surface. Knead for 10 minutes until smooth and elastic. Put in the prepared bowl, cover and leave to rise in a warm place for 1 hour until doubled in size.

**Put** a heavy-based baking sheet on the middle shelf of a preheated oven, 230°C (450°F), Gas Mark 8, and heat for 5 minutes. Meanwhile, mix the passata, pesto and salt together in a bowl.

**Knock** the air out of the dough. Divide in half. Roll one half out to a 25 cm (10 inch) round. Transfer to the heated baking sheet. Spread half the passata mixture over the pizza base. Top with half the taleggio slices and asparagus and drizzle with half the oil. Bake for 10–15 minutes until the base is crisp and golden. Season with pepper and serve immediately. Repeat to make the second pizza.

**For artichoke & buffalo mozzarella pizza**, use the same quantity of ready-made green pesto instead of red pesto. Slice 250 g (8 oz) buffalo mozzarella and use in place of the taleggio and replace the asparagus with the same quantity of drained bottled or canned artichoke hearts in oil. If you can only find large asparagus spears, halve them lengthways before scattering over the pizza. Finish the recipe as above.

# goats' cheese flatbread pizza

Makes **4**

Preparation time **10 minutes**

Cooking time **7–8 minutes**

4 x 20 cm (8 inch)
  **Mediterranean flatbreads**
2 tablespoons **sun-dried
  tomato paste**
300 g (10 oz) **mozzarella
  cheese**, sliced
6 **plum tomatoes**, roughly
  chopped
4 tablespoons **olive oil**
1 **garlic clove**, crushed
small handful of **basil leaves**,
  roughly torn
100 g (3½ oz) **soft goats'
  cheese**
**salt and black pepper**

**Lay** the flatbreads on 2 baking sheets and spread with the sun-dried tomato paste. Top with the mozzarella slices and bake in a preheated oven, 200°C (400°F), Gas Mark 6, for 7–8 minutes, until the bases are crisp and the cheese has melted.

**Meanwhile**, put the tomatoes in a bowl, add the oil, garlic and basil and season generously with salt and pepper.

**Divide** the tomato mixture between the flatbreads and crumble over the goats' cheese. Serve immediately.

**For easy roasted pepper pizza**, replace the plum tomatoes with 4 sun-dried tomatoes in oil, drained and roughly chopped, combined with 200 g (7 oz) drained bottled roasted peppers, and use chopped oregano instead of the basil. After adding the goats' cheese, scatter the flatbreads with a few pitted black olives and serve.

# desserts

# rich chocolate mousse

Serves **4**
Preparation time **5 minutes**,
 plus chilling
Cooking time **3–4 minutes**

175 g (6 oz) **plain dark
 chocolate**, broken into
 pieces
100 ml (3 fl oz) **double cream**
3 **eggs**, separated
**cocoa powder**, for dusting

**Put** the chocolate and cream in a heatproof bowl set
over a saucepan of gently simmering water (do not let
the bowl touch the water) and stir until the chocolate
has melted. Leave to cool for 5 minutes, then beat in
the egg yolks one at a time.

**Whisk** the egg whites in a separate clean bowl until
stiff, then lightly fold into the chocolate mixture
until combined. Spoon the mousse into 4 dessert
glasses or cups and chill for 2 hours. Dust with cocoa
powder before serving.

**For chocolate & orange mousse**, follow the recipe
above but add the grated rind of 1 large orange and
2 tablespoons Grand Marnier to the melted chocolate
and cream. Continue the recipe as above.

# poached apricots with pistachios

Serves **4**

Preparation time **10 minutes**,
  plus chilling and cooling

Cooking time **8 minutes**

125 g (4 oz) **caster sugar**

300 ml (½ pint) **water**

2 strips of **lemon rind**

2 **cardamom pods**

1 **vanilla pod**

12 **apricots**, halved and
  stoned

1 tablespoon **lemon juice**

1 tablespoon **rosewater**

25 g (1 oz) **pistachio nuts**,
  finely chopped

**vanilla ice cream or Greek-
  style yogurt**, to serve
  (optional)

**Put** a large bowl in the freezer to chill. Put the sugar and measurement water in a wide saucepan and heat over a low heat until the sugar has dissolved. Meanwhile, cut the lemon rind into fine strips, crush the cardamom pods and split the vanilla pod in half. Add the lemon rind, cardamom and vanilla pod to the pan.

**Add** the apricots and simmer gently for 5 minutes, or until softened. Remove from the heat, add the lemon juice and rosewater and transfer to the chilled bowl. Leave to cool until required.

**Spoon** the apricots and a little of the syrup into serving bowls, scatter over the pistachio nuts and serve with ice cream or Greek-style yogurt, if you like.

**For poached peaches with almonds**, follow the first stage of the recipe above, but replace the lemon rind with orange rind and the cardamom pods with ½ cinnamon stick. Peel, halve and stone 4 large peaches, then poach until softened and add orange juice and orange flower water in place of the lemon juice and rosewater. After cooling, serve scattered with toasted flaked almonds instead of the pistachio nuts.

# apple fritters with blackberry sauce

Serves **4**

Preparation time **15 minutes**

Cooking time **about 10 minutes**

2 **eggs**

125 g (4 oz) **plain flour**

4 tablespoons **caster sugar**

150 ml (¼ pint) **milk**

**sunflower oil**, for deep-frying

4 **dessert apples**, cored and thickly sliced

150 g (5 oz) **frozen blackberries**

2 tablespoons **water**

**icing sugar**, for dusting

**Separate** one egg and put the white into one bowl and the yolk and the whole egg into a second bowl. Add the flour and half the caster sugar to the second bowl. Whisk the egg white until if forms soft peaks, then use the same whisk to beat the flour mixture until smooth, gradually whisking in the milk. Fold in the egg white.

**Pour** the oil into a deep, heavy-based saucepan until it comes one-third of the way up the side, then heat until it reaches 180–190°C (350–375°F), or until a cube of bread browns in 30 seconds. Dip a few apple slices in the batter and turn gently to coat. Lift out one slice at a time and lower carefully into the oil. Deep-fry, in batches, for 2–3 minutes, turning until evenly golden. Remove with a slotted spoon and drain on kitchen paper.

**Meanwhile**, put the blackberries, remaining sugar and measurement water in a small saucepan and heat for 2–3 minutes until hot. Arrange the fritters on serving plates, spoon the blackberry sauce around and dust with a little icing sugar.

**For banana fritters with raspberry sauce**, use 4 thickly sliced bananas in place of the apples. Use 150 g (5 oz) raspberries instead of the blackberries. Continue with the recipe as above.

# caramel apple crumble

Serves **4**

Preparation time **15 minutes**

Cooking time **25 minutes**

**spray oil**, for oiling

750 g (1½ lb) **Bramley cooking apples**

75 g (3 oz) **unsalted butter**, diced, plus extra for greasing

3 tablespoons **soft light brown sugar**

6 whole **cloves**

50 g (2 oz) **sultanas**

75 ml (3 fl oz) **cold water**

**For the crumble topping**

75 g (3 oz) **rolled oats**

75 g (3 oz) **plain flour**

50 g (2 oz) **ground hazelnuts**

50 g (2 oz) **soft light brown sugar**

2 teaspoons **ground cinnamon**

100 g (3½ oz) **unsalted butter**, diced

**Lightly** oil 4 x 300 ml (½ pint) individual baking dishes or cups with spray oil. Peel, core and thickly slice the apples and put in a saucepan with the butter, sugar, cloves, sultanas and measurement water. Cover and cook over a low heat for 5–6 minutes until the apples are just softened. Divide between the prepared dishes or cups.

**Put** the oats, flour, ground hazelnuts, sugar and cinnamon in a bowl and stir well until combined. Add the butter and rub in with the fingertips until the mixture resembles coarse breadcrumbs. Spoon the crumble topping over the apple mixture and bake in a preheated oven, 190°C (375°F), Gas Mark 5, for 25 minutes until bubbling and golden.

**For peach & blueberry crumble**, replace the apples with 450 g (14½ oz) halved, stoned and sliced peaches and 250 g (8 oz) blueberries, and cook as in the first stage above with 25 g (1 oz) butter, 2 tablespoons caster sugar and 2 tablespoons cold water until just softened. Continue with the recipe as above.

# soufflé jam omelette

Serves **4**
Preparation time **10 minutes**
Cooking time **8–12 minutes**

6 **eggs**, separated
2 teaspoons **vanilla extract**
4 tablespoons **icing sugar**
40 g (1½ oz) **butter**
4 tablespoons **raspberry jam**
100 g (3½ oz) **raspberries**,
   defrosted if frozen
100 g (3½ oz) **blueberries**,
   defrosted if frozen
**single cream**, to serve

**Whisk** the egg whites in a large bowl until they form soft peaks. Put the yolks, vanilla extract and 1 tablespoon of the sugar in a separate bowl and use the same whisk to beat them together. Fold a spoonful of the egg whites into the yolks to loosen the mixture, then add the remainder and fold in gently with a large metal spoon.

**Melt** half the butter in a 20 cm (8 inch) frying pan. As soon as it stops foaming, swirl in half the egg mixture and cook over a medium heat for 3–4 minutes until the underside is golden, then transfer to a preheated hot grill to brown the top lightly. Carefully slide the omelette on to a warmed serving plate and keep warm in a moderate oven. Repeat with the remaining ingredients to make a second omelette.

**Dot** the omelettes with the jam and berries, then fold in half to enclose the filling. Dust the tops with the remaining sugar, cut in half and serve immediately with cream.

**For soufflé marmalade omelette**, use the same quantity of orange marmalade instead of the jam. Peel 4 oranges, cutting off all the pith around the fruit. Remove the segments and discard the membrane and seeds. Arrange the segments, whole or halved on the omelette with the orange marmalade.

# grilled fruits with palm sugar

Serves **4**
Preparation time **10 minutes**
Cooking time **6–16 minutes**

25 g (1 oz) **palm sugar**
grated rind and juice of
  1 **lime**
2 tablespoons **water**
½ teaspoon cracked **black
  peppercorns**
500 g (1 lb) **mixed prepared
  fruits**, such as pineapple
  or peach slices or mango
  wedges

**To serve**
**cinnamon** or **vanilla ice
  cream**
**lime slices**

**Put** the sugar, lime rind and juice, measurement water
and peppercorns in a small saucepan and heat over a
low heat until the sugar has dissolved. Plunge the base
of the pan into iced water to cool.

**Brush** the cooled syrup over the prepared fruits and
cook under a preheated hot grill for 6–8 minutes on
each side, or over a preheated hot gas barbecue or the
hot coals of a charcoal barbecue, for 3–4 minutes on
each side until charred and tender.

**Serve** with scoops of cinnamon or vanilla ice cream
and lime slices.

**For grilled fruit kebabs**, cut the prepared fruits
into large chunks, thread on to wooden skewers,
presoaked in cold water for 30 minutes, and brush
with the cooled syrup before cooking as in the
recipe above.

# tiramisù cheesecake

Serves **8–12**
Preparation time **20 minutes**,
  plus chilling
Cooking time **50 minutes–**
  **1 hour**

**spray oil**, for oiling
16 **Savoiardi biscuits** (see
  page 12)
4 tablespoons cold
  **espresso coffee**
500 g (1 lb) **cream cheese**
250 g (8 oz) **mascarpone**
  **cheese**
3 **eggs**
125 g (4 oz) **caster sugar**
2 tablespoons **Marsala**
25 g (1 oz) **plain dark**
  **chocolate**

**Lightly** oil a 23 cm (9 inch) square cake tin with spray oil and line with nonstick baking paper, allowing the paper to overhang the edges. Arrange the Savoiardi biscuits, sugar-side up, in the base of the tin, trimming them to fit, if necessary. Brush the biscuits with the coffee.

**Put** the cream cheese, mascarpone, eggs, sugar and Marsala in a clean a bowl. Using an electric whisk, beat together until smooth, then pour into the prepared tin and smooth the surface. Grate over the chocolate to cover the surface of the cake.

**Bake** in a preheated oven, 140°C (275°F), Gas Mark 1, for 50 minutes–1 hour until firm. Leave to cool, then chill for 1 hour. Carefully remove the cheesecake from the tin and cut into slices.

**For chocolate cheesecake**, melt 125 g (4 oz) plain dark chocolate, broken into pieces, in a heatproof bowl set over a saucepan of gently simmering water. Follow the recipe above, folding the melted chocolate into the cheese mixture along with 2 tablespoons sifted cocoa powder. Bake as above.

# strawberry & lavender crush

Serves **4**
Preparation time **10 minutes**

400 g (13 oz) fresh
  **strawberries**
2 tablespoons **icing sugar**,
  plus extra for dusting
4–5 **lavender flower stems**,
  plus extra to decorate
400 g (13 oz) **Greek-style
  yogurt**
4 ready-made **meringue
  nests**

**Reserve** 4 small strawberries for decoration. Hull the remainder, put in a bowl with the sugar and mash together with a fork. Alternatively, process the strawberries and sugar in a food processor or blender to a smooth purée. Pull off the lavender flowers from the stems and crumble them into the purée to taste.

**Put** the yogurt in a bowl, crumble in the meringues, then lightly mix together. Add the strawberry purée and fold together with a spoon until marbled. Spoon into 4 dessert glasses.

**Cut** the reserved strawberries in half, then use together with the lavender flowers to decorate the desserts. Lightly dust with icing sugar and serve immediately.

**For peach & rosewater crush**, peel, halve and stone 3 peaches, then roughly chop and mash or process in a food processor or blender with 2 tablespoons clear honey and 2 teaspoons rosewater. Continue with the recipe as above, but decorate the desserts with crystallized rose petals.

# summer berry sorbet

Serves **2**

Preparation time **5 minutes**, plus freezing

250 g (8 oz) **frozen mixed summer berries**

75 ml (3 fl oz) **spiced berry cordial**

2 tablespoons **Kirsch**

1 tablespoon **lime juice**

**Put** a shallow plastic container in the freezer to chill. Process the frozen berries, cordial, Kirsch and lime juice in a food processor or blender to a smooth purée. Be careful not to over-process, as this will soften the mixture too much.

**Spoon** into the chilled container and freeze for at least 25 minutes. Spoon into serving bowls and serve.

**For raspberry sorbet**, replace the main recipe ingredients with frozen raspberries, elderflower cordial, crème de cassis and lemon juice. Use the same quantities and method as the summer berry sorbet.

# banana & fig filo pastry

Serves **4**

Preparation time **15 minutes**

Cooking time **15 minutes**

6 large sheets of **filo pastry**

50 g (2 oz) **unsalted butter**, melted

4 **bananas**, sliced

6 **dried figs**, sliced

25 g (1 oz) **caster sugar**

grated rind of ½ **lemon**

½ teaspoon ground **cinnamon**

**thick double cream** or **Greek-style yogurt**, to serve

**Cut** the pastry sheets in half crossways. Lay one sheet flat on a baking sheet and brush with melted butter, top with a second sheet and again brush with melted butter. Repeat with the remaining sheets.

**Arrange** the banana and fig slices over the pastry. Combine the sugar, lemon rind and cinnamon, then sprinkle over the fruit and drizzle over any remaining melted butter.

**Bake** in a preheated oven, 200°C (400°F), Gas Mark 6, for 15 minutes until the pastry is crisp and the fruit golden. Serve hot with cream or Greek-style yogurt.

**For spiced apple filo pastry**, prepare the filo pastry base as in the recipe above. Core and quarter 2 apples and cut into wafer-thin slices. Arrange the slices over the pastry in overlapping rows. Drizzle over 25 g (1 oz) melted butter and sprinkle with 2 tablespoons caster sugar mixed with 1 teaspoon ground cinnamon. Bake as above for 20 minutes.

# bananas with toffee sauce

Serves **4**
Preparation time **5 minutes**
Cooking time **5 minutes**

4 **bananas**
125 g (4 oz) **unsalted butter**
**ground cinnamon or freshly**
  **grated nutmeg**, to
  decorate (optional)
**vanilla ice cream**, to serve

**For the toffee sauce**
125 g (4 oz) **palm sugar**
125 ml (4 fl oz) **double cream**
**lime juice**, to taste

**Peel** the bananas and cut into quarters or in half lengthways. Melt the butter in a frying pan, add the bananas and cook over a medium-high heat for about 30 seconds on each side until lightly golden. Remove with a slotted spoon and transfer to a warmed dish.

**Stir** the sugar and cream into the pan and heat over a low heat until the sugar has dissolved. Simmer gently for 2–3 minutes until thickened. Add lime juice to taste.

**Serve** the bananas drizzled with the toffee sauce and with a scoop of vanilla ice cream. Sprinkle with cinnamon or nutmeg to decorate, if you like.

**For pineapple with toffee sauce**, peel a ripe fresh pineapple, removing the 'eyes', then slice into rings. Lay the rings on a chopping board and remove the central cores with an apple corer. Cook the pineapple rings in the same way as the bananas and continue with the recipe as above.

# caramelized clementines

Serves **4**

Preparation time **10 minutes**,
  plus cooling

Cooking time **15 minutes**

250 g (8 oz) **granulated
  sugar**

250 ml (8 fl oz) **cold water**

6 tablespoons **boiling water**

8 **clementines**, peeled

3 whole **star anise**

**cream or crème fraîche**,
  to serve

**Put** the sugar and cold measurement water in a small saucepan and heat over a low heat, without stirring, until the sugar has completely dissolved. Don't be tempted to stir the mixture or the sugar will harden – tilt the pan to mix the sugar, if needed. Increase the heat and boil for 10 minutes, or until just turning pale golden.

**Remove** the pan from the heat and add the boiling measurement water, a tablespoon at a time, standing well back after each addition as it will spit. Tilt the pan to mix, heating gently if needed.

**Put** the clementines in a heatproof bowl with the star anise, then pour over the hot syrup and leave to cool for 3–4 hours. Stir the clementines and transfer to a serving dish. Serve with cream or crème fraîche.

**For herb-scented caramelized clementines**, use 3 fresh rosemary sprigs or 2 bay leaves instead of the star anise. Tuck the herbs under the clementines in the dish before adding the syrup.

# brioche pudding with ice cream

Serves **4**

Preparation time **45 minutes**, plus infusing, cooling, freezing and soaking

Cooking time **40 minutes**

8 slices of **brioche**

3 **eggs**, lightly beaten

50 g (2 oz) **caster sugar**

250 ml (8 fl oz) **milk**

250 ml (8 fl oz) **double cream**

½ teaspoon ground **mixed spice**

25 g (1 oz) **butter**, melted

1 tablespoon **demerara sugar**

**For the ice cream**

750 ml (1¼ pints) **double cream**

1 **vanilla pod**, split

5 **egg yolks**

125 ml (4 fl oz) **maple syrup**

**First** make the ice cream. Put the cream and vanilla pod in a saucepan and heat to boiling point. Remove from the heat and leave to infuse for 20 minutes. Scrape the seeds from the pod into the cream.

**Beat** the egg yolks and maple syrup together in a bowl, stir in the cream and return to the pan. Heat gently, stirring, until the custard thickens to coat the back of a wooden spoon. Don't allow to boil. Leave to cool. Freeze in a plastic container, beating every hour, for 5 hours, or until frozen.

**Cut** the brioche slices diagonally into quarters to form triangles. Arrange, overlapping, in 4 x 250 ml (8 fl oz) baking dishes. Whisk the eggs, caster sugar, milk, cream and spice in a separate bowl. Pour over the brioche slices, pushing them down so that they are almost covered. Drizzle over the butter and scatter over the demerara sugar. Leave to soak for 30 minutes.

**Set** the baking dishes in a large roasting tin. Pour in enough boiling water to come halfway up the sides of the dishes. Bake in a preheated oven, 180°C (350°F), Gas Mark 4, for 30 minutes until set and the top is lightly golden. Serve with the ice cream.

**For classic bread & butter pudding**, replace the brioche slices with white bread. Butter one side, cut diagonally in half and arrange in a 1.5 litre (2½ pint) baking dish. Pour over the custard and bake for 45–50 minutes until set.

# orange palmiers with plums

Serves **4**

Preparation time **20 minutes**

Cooking time **10 minutes**

1 sheet of ready-rolled frozen
  **puff pastry**, about 25 cm
  (10 inches) square,
  defrosted
1 **egg**, beaten
3 tablespoons **light
  muscovado sugar**
finely grated rind of ½ **orange**
**spray oil**, for oiling
6 tablespoons **orange juice**
50 g (2 oz) **caster sugar**
400 g (13 oz) **plums**, stoned
  and sliced
**icing sugar**, for dusting
**crème fraîche**, to serve

**Brush** the pastry with some of the beaten egg,
then sprinkle with the muscovado sugar and orange
rind. Roll one edge of the pastry until it reaches the
centre. Do the same from the opposite edge until
both rolls meet.

**Brush** the pastry with more beaten egg, then cut into
8 thick slices. Lightly oil a baking sheet with spray oil.
Arrange the pastry slices, cut side-up, on the prepared
baking sheet. Bake in a preheated oven, 200°C
(400°F), Gas Mark 6, for 10 minutes until well risen
and golden.

**Meanwhile**, put the orange juice and caster sugar
in a saucepan. Add the plums and cook, stirring, over
a medium heat for 5 minutes.

**Sandwich** the palmiers together in pairs with the
plums, dust with icing sugar and serve with a spoonful
of crème fraîche.

**For seasonal fruit palmiers**, instead of plums, use
the best seasonal ingredients. Chop 450 g (14½ oz)
fresh rhubarb, or stone and slice 400 g (13 oz)
greengages. Use 450 g (14½ oz) raspberries,
according to availability. Continue the recipe as above.

# very berry fruit salad

Serves **4**

Preparation time **10 minutes**, plus cooling

Cooking time **10 minutes**

3 **oranges**
50 g (2 oz) **granulated sugar**
1 **vanilla pod**, split
1 **cinnamon stick**, lightly bruised
250 g (8 oz) fresh **strawberries**
200 g (7 oz) fresh **cherries**
125 g (4 oz) fresh **raspberries**
125 g (4 oz) fresh **blueberries**

**Squeeze** the juice from the oranges into a measuring jug and make up to 300 ml (½ pint) with cold water. Put in a saucepan with the sugar, vanilla pod and cinnamon stick. Heat over a low heat, stirring, until the sugar has dissolved, then simmer gently for 5 minutes until a light syrup is reached.

**Remove** from the heat and leave to cool completely. Remove the vanilla pod and cinnamon stick.

**Hull** and halve the strawberries, then put in a large bowl with the remaining berries and pour over the syrup. Stir well and leave to marinate at room temperature for 30 minutes.

**For fragrant berry & rosewater salad**, put 300 ml (½ pint) cold water in a saucepan with 75 g (3 oz) caster sugar and 1 lightly bruised cinnamon stick. Heat over a low heat, stirring, until the sugar has dissolved, then simmer for 5 minutes. Remove the cinnamon stick, then take the saucepan off the heat and leave to cool. Stir in 1 tablespoon rosewater and the berries.

# cherry & cinnamon zabaglione

Serves **4**
Preparation time **10 minutes**
Cooking time **12–15 minutes**

4 **egg yolks**
125 g (4 oz) **caster sugar**
150 ml (¼ pint) **cream sherry**
large pinch of ground
   **cinnamon**
425 g (14 oz) can **black
   cherries** in syrup
2 **amaretti biscuits**,
   crumbled, to decorate

**Pour** 5 cm (2 inches) of water into a medium saucepan and bring to the boil. Cover with a large heatproof bowl, making sure that the water does not touch the base of the bowl. Reduce the heat so that the water is simmering, then add the egg yolks, sugar, sherry and cinnamon to the bowl. Whisk for 5–8 minutes until very thick and foamy, and the custard leaves a trail when the whisk is lifted above the mixture.

**Drain** off some of the cherry syrup and then tip the cherries and just a little of the syrup into a small saucepan. Warm through, then spoon into 4 dessert glasses.

**Pour** the warm zabaglione over the top and decorate with the amaretti biscuits. Serve immediately.

**For apricot & vanilla zabaglione**, replace the sherry with Marsala, omit the cinnamon and add 2 drops vanilla extract and the grated rind of ½ lemon to the egg yolks. Use canned apricots instead of the black cherries. Continue the recipe as above.

# rhubarb, pear & marzipan crumble

Serves **4**
Preparation time **20 minutes**
Cooking time **35–40 minutes**

400 g (13 oz) **trimmed rhubarb**, thinly sliced
1 ripe **pear**, peeled, cored and sliced
100 g (3½ oz) **caster sugar**
125 g (4 oz) **plain flour**
50 g (2 oz) **butter**, diced
125 g (4 oz) **marzipan**, coarsely grated
**flaked almonds**, for sprinkling
**custard**, to serve

**Put** the rhubarb and pear into a 1.2 litre (2 pint) ovenproof pie dish with half the sugar.

**Put** the remaining sugar in a food processor, add the flour and butter and process until the mixture resembles fine breadcrumbs. Alternatively, put the ingredients into a bowl, add the butter and rub in with the fingertips until the mixture resembles fine breadcrumbs. Stir in the marzipan.

**Spoon** over the fruit and sprinkle with a few flaked almonds. Cook in a preheated oven, 180°C (350°F), Gas Mark 4, for 35–40 minutes until golden brown, checking after 15–20 minutes and covering with foil to prevent over-browning if necessary. Serve hot with custard.

**For plum, apple & marzipan crumble**, replace the rhubarb with 500 g (1 lb) halved, stoned ripe plums and the pear with a large peeled, cored and sliced Bramley cooking apple. Continue the recipe as above. The crumble mix can be made in bulk and stored in a plastic bag in the freezer until needed.

# sweet wonton millefeuille

Makes **12**
Preparation time **10 minutes**,
   plus cooling
Cooking time **3 minutes**

2 tablespoons **caster sugar**
½ teaspoon ground
   **cinnamon**
9 **wonton wrappers**
25 g (1 oz) **unsalted butter**,
   melted
125 g (4 oz) **mascarpone
   cheese**
1–2 tablespoons **icing sugar**,
   plus extra for dusting
1 teaspoon **lemon juice**
125 g (4 oz) fresh
   **strawberries**, hulled and
   sliced

**Mix** the caster sugar and cinnamon together. Cut the wonton wrappers into quarters, brush with the melted butter and coat with a layer of the spiced sugar.

**Put** on a baking sheet and bake in a preheated oven, 200°C (400°F), Gas Mark 6, for 2–3 minutes until crisp and golden. Leave to cool on a wire rack.

**Beat** the mascarpone with the icing sugar and lemon juice in a bowl and spread a little over 12 of the crisp wontons. Top with half the strawberry slices. Repeat the process with another 12 wontons and the remaining mascarpone mixture and strawberries to make a second layer. Put the remaining wontons on top and dust with a little extra icing sugar. Serve with glasses of champagne, if you like.

**For sweet berry millefeuille,** use raspberries or blackberries instead of the strawberries, and replace the mascarpone with 150 g (5 oz) crème fraîche.

# index

**almonds:** Poached peaches with almonds 202
Watercress, almond & Stilton salad 152
apples: Apple fritters with blackberry sauce 204
Caramel apple crumble 206
Plum, apple & marzipan crumble 232
Spiced apple filo pastry 218
Spiced apple sauce 32
apricots: Apricot & vanilla zabaglione 230
Apricot purée 34
Poached apricots with pistachios 202
Artichoke & buffalo mozzarella pizza 194
asparagus: Asparagus & taleggio pizza 194
Asparagus, tomato & feta frittata 102
Boiled egg with asparagus 20
Charred asparagus salad with pine nuts 142
Summer pea & asparagus soup 118
aubergines: Aubergine & goats' cheese gratin 186
Aubergine buck rarebit 86
Aubergine dip with flatbreads 60
Aubergine lasagne 186
Aubergine and mozzarella panini 48
Aubergine toasties with pesto 86
Aubergine and tomato curry 104

Grilled vegetables & couscous 76
Saffron-scented vegetable tagine 128
avocadoes: Avocado salsa 42
Italian tricolore salad 140
Tomato, avocado & peach salad 140

**bananas:** Banana & fig filo pastry 218
Banana fritters with blackberry sauce 204
Bananas with toffee sauce 220
beans: Bean, lemon & rosemary hummus 68
Broad bean & lemon spaghetti 82
Broad bean and dill pesto 52
Chilli bean soup 114
Fig, bean & toasted pecan salad 156
Home baked beans 136
Mixed bean salad 156
Mushroom, flageolet & tomato lasagne 90
Pasta & bean soup with basil oil 124
Spiced tomato and Mexican bean soup 124
Vegetable tempura 164
beetroot: Beetroot & goats' cheese risotto 88
Beetroot & mascarpone risotto with pine nuts 88
berries: Fragrant berry and rosewater salad 228
Honeyed ricotta with summer fruits 34
Summer berry sorbet 216

Sweet berry millefeuille 234
Blackberry sauce 204
blueberries: Blueberry sauce 32
Peach and blueberry crumble 206
Soufflé jam omelette 208
Very berry fruit salad 228
bread: Aubergine toasties with pesto 86
Bread and butter pudding 224
Brioche pudding with ice cream 224
Bruschetta with fig, rocket and feta 50
Bruschetta with tomatoes & ricotta 50
Chilli & sweetcorn cornbread 182
Crostini with pea & ricotta pesto 52
Herb & cheese damper 184
Middle Eastern bread salad 148
Mixed seed soda bread 180
Parmesan eggy bread 16
Pinhead oatmeal soda bread 180
Sweet eggy bread 16
Tomato & bread salad 148
Brioche pudding with ice cream 224
broccoli: Stir-fried tofu with basil & chilli 98
Vegetable tempura 164
Bruschetta: with fig, rocket and feta 50
with tomatoes & ricotta 50
butter: Gnocchi with sage butter 46

Soft polenta with sage butter 170
Truffle butter 112

**cannelloni** see pasta
Caramel apple crumble 206
carrots: Curried carrot & lentil soup 110
Roast vegetables & parsley pesto 160
Spiced carrot and tomato soup 110
Winter vegetable and lentil tagine 128
Winter vegetables & beer broth 120
cashew nuts: Potato, chickpea & cashew curry 104
celeriac: Vegetable & rice soup 120
cheese 9, 12
Artichoke & buffalo mozzarella pizza 194
Asparagus & taleggio pizza 194
Asparagus, tomato & feta frittata 102
Aubergine & goats' cheese gratin 186
Aubergine buck rarebit 86
Aubergine lasagne 186
Aubergine and mozzarella panini 48
Aubergine toasties with pesto 86
Baked figs with goats' cheese 56
Beetroot & goats' cheese risotto 88
Beetroot & mascarpone risotto with pine nuts 88
Bruschetta with fig, rocket and feta 50
Bruschetta with tomatoes & ricotta 50

Cheese & tomato omelette 18

Cheese, tomato & basil muffins 24

Cheesy scrambled eggs 26

Cherry tomato and cheese pizza 190

Colourful, cheesy roasted pepper 78

Creamy pea & mint risotto with brie 80

Crostini with pea & ricotta pesto 52

Field mushrooms and Camembert on toast 30

Fig, goats' cheese & tapenade tart 174

Figs stuffed with mozzarella and basil 56

Four cheese pizza 190

Goats' cheese flatbread pizza 196

Greek country salad with haloumi 154

Grilled vegetable & goats' cheese tart 174

Haloumi with pomegranate salsa 42

Herb & cheese damper 184

Honeyed ricotta with summer fruits 34

Italian tricolore salad 140

Leek & thyme burgers with blue cheese 84

Onion and goats' cheese tart 70

Onion, walnut & blue cheese tarts 70

Parmesan eggy bread 16

Pumpkin and ricotta cannelloni 100

Roasted squash & sage pizza 192

Rocket & goats' cheese omelette 18

Sage & goats' cheese frittata 54

Spinach & feta tart 176

Spinach & Gorgonzola salad 152

Spinach & ricotta cannelloni 100

Spinach and goats' cheese frittata 54

Sweet potato & fontana panini 48

Sweet wonton millefeuille 234

Tiramisù cheesecake 212

Tomato & feta tart 178

Watercress, almond & Stilton salad 152

Watermelon, fennel & feta salad 144

cheesecakes: Chocolate cheesecake 212

Tiramisù cheesecake 212

cherries: Cherry & cinnamon zabaglione 230

Very berry fruit salad 228

chickpeas: Chickpea and chilli hummus 68

Felafel pitta pockets 62

Potato, chickpea & cashew curry 104

Saffron-scented vegetable tagine 128

chilli: Chilli bean soup 114

Stir-fried tofu with basil & chilli 98

Szechuan chilli dressing 66

chillies: Chickpea and chilli hummus 68

Chilli & sweetcorn cornbread 182

Chilli vinegar dressing 58

Chive dumplings 130

chocolate: Chocolate & orange mousse 200

Chocolate cheesecake 212

Chocolate walnut muffins 38

Rich chocolate mousse 200

Triple chocolate muffins 38

Citrus croissants, Spiced 36

Clementines, Caramelized 222

coconut milk: Creamy pumpkin, coriander and coconut soup 122

Sweet potato & coconut soup 122

courgettes: Grilled vegetables & couscous 76

Vegetable kebabs with pilaf 94

Vegetable tempura 164

couscous: Couscous tabbouleh 146

Grilled vegetables & couscous 76

Spiced couscous salad 146

Croissants 36

cucumber: Couscous tabbouleh 146

Cucumber and mint dip 60

Greek country salad with haloumi 154

Middle Eastern bread salad 148

**Dumplings** 130

**eggs** 11

All-in-one veggie breakfast 22

Apricot & vanilla

zabaglione 230

Asparagus, tomato & feta frittata 102

Boiled egg with asparagus 20

Boiled egg with mustard soldiers 20

Cheese & tomato omelette 18

Cheesy scrambled eggs 26

Cherry & cinnamon zabaglione 230

Ice cream 224

Mixed mushroom frittata 102

Omelette with basil tomatoes 92

Pancakes with blueberry sauce 32

Pancakes with spcied apple sauce 32

Parmesan eggy bread 16

Pesto scrambled eggs 26

Potato rösti with frazzled eggs 28

Potato rösti with poached eggs 28

Rich chocolate mousse 200

Rocket & goats' cheese omelette 18

Sage & goats' cheese frittata 54

Soufflé jam omelette 208

Soufflé marmalade omelette 208

Spinach and goats' cheese frittata 54

Sweet eggy bread 16

Tomato stuffed omelette 92

**fennel:** Fennel gratin 134

Fennel, orange and parsley salad 144

Fennel, Pernod & orange casserole 134
Provençal vegetable stew 132
Watermelon, fennel & feta salad 144
figs: Baked figs with goats' cheese 56
Banana & fig filo pastry 218
Bruschetta with fig, rocket and feta 50
Fig, bean & toasted pecan salad 156
Fig, goats' cheese & tapenade tart 174
Figs stuffed with mozzarella and basil 56
Saffron-scented vegetable tagine 128
frittata see eggs

**garlic:** Garlic mayonnaise 76
Roasted new potatoes with garlic & rosemary 162
ginger: Mushroom & ginger wontons 66
gnocchi: Gnocchi, plum tomato & sage butter gratin 46
Gnocchi with sage butter 46
Gnocchi with walnut pesto 64
Goulash with chive dumplings 130
grapefruit: Spiced citrus croissants 36

**hazelnuts,** Charred leek salad with 142
Honeyed ricotta with summer fruits 34
Horseradish dumplings 130
hummus: Bean, lemon &

rosemary 68
Chickpea and chilli 68

**kaffir** lime leaves 13
Sweetcorn & kaffir lime fritters 44

**lasagne** see pasta
lavender: Strawberry & lavender crush 214
leeks: Charred leek salad with hazelnuts 142
Leek & thyme burgers with blue cheese 84
Leek & thyme sausages with relish 84
lemons: Bean, lemon & rosemary hummus 68
Broad bean & lemon spaghetti 82
lentils: Curried carrot & lentil soup 110
Winter vegetable and lentil tagine 128

**marsala** 13
marzipan: Plum, apple & marzipan crumble 232
Rhubarb, pear & marzipan crumble 232
Millefeuille 123
mirin 13
Mousses 200
muffins: Cheese, tomato & basil 24
Chilli & sweetcorn 182
Chocolate walnut 38
Olive and pine nut 24
Triple chocolate 38
mushrooms: All-in-one veggie breakfast 22
Asian-style risotto 96
Crispy mushroom wontons 66
Field mushrooms and Camembert on toast 30
Italian-style risotto 96

Mixed mushroom frittata 102
Mixed mushroom tart 176
Mixed mushrooms on toast 30
Mushroom & ginger wontons 66
Mushroom, flageolet & tomato lasagne 90
Mushroom ramen 126
Mushroom soup with truffle butter 112
Mushroom, walnut & thyme soup 112
Saffron-scented vegetable tagine 128
Spinach & mushroom lasagne 90
Vegetable kebabs with pilaf 94

**noodles** 12
Mushroom ramen 126
Vegetable ramen 126

**oatmeal:** Pinhead oatmeal soda bread 180
olives: Olive and pine nut muffins 24
Olive salsa 116
Provençal vegetable stew 132
omelettes see eggs
oranges: Fennel, orange and parsley salad 144
Fennel, Pernod & orange casserole 134
Orange palmiers with plums 226
Soufflé marmalade omelette 208
Spiced citrus croissants 36

**pancakes** see eggs
parsnips: Potato & parsnip gratin 188

Roast vegetables & parsley pesto 160
Winter vegetables & beer broth 120
pasta: Aubergine lasagne 186
Broad bean & lemon spaghetti 82
Mushroom, flageolet & tomato lasagne 90
Pasta & bean soup with basil oil 124
Pasta with parsley pesto 160
Pasta with Provençal sauce 132
Pumpkin and ricotta cannelloni 100
Spaghetti with peas and mint 82
Spinach & mushroom lasagne 90
Spinach & ricotta cannelloni 100
peaches: Peach & rosewater crush 214
Peach and blueberry crumble 206
Poached peaches with almonds 202
Tomato, avocado & peach salad 140
pears: Rhubarb, pear & marzipan crumble 232
peas: Butternut squash, tofu & pea curry 74
Creamy pea & mint risotto with brie 80
Crostini with pea & ricotta pesto 52
Pea, potato & rocket soup 118
Spaghetti with peas and mint 82
Stir-fried tofu with basil & chilli 98
Summer pea & asparagus soup 118
pecan nuts: Fig, bean &

toasted pecan salad
156
peppers: Colourful,
cheesy roasted pepper
78
Easy roasted pepper
pizza 196
Grilled vegetables &
couscous 76
Middle Eastern bread
salad 148
Provençal vegetable
stew 132
Roasted stuffed
peppers 78
Vegetable kebabs with
pilaf 94
Vegetable tempura 164
Pesto 86
Aubergine toasties with
pesto 86
Parsley pesto 160
Pasta with parsley
pesto 160
Pea & ricotta pesto 52
Pesto scrambled eggs
26
Walnut pesto 64
pine nuts: Beetroot &
mascarpone risotto with
pine nuts 88
Charred asparagus
salad with pine nuts
142
New potato, basil &
pine nut salad 150
Olive and pine nut
muffins 24
Potato gratin with pine
nut crust 188
Pineapple with toffee
sauce 220
pistachios, Poached
apricots with 202
pitta breads: Felafel pitta
pockets 62
plums: Orange palmiers
with plums 226
Plum, apple & marzipan
crumble 232

polenta 12
Chargrilled polenta
triangles 170
Soft polenta with sage
butter 170
pomegranates: Haloumi
with pomegranate salsa
42
Ponzu dipping sauce 164
potatoes: All-in-one
veggie breakfast 22
Gnocchi, plum tomato &
sage butter gratin 46
Gnocchi with sage
butter 46
Goulash with chive
dumplings 130
Home baked beans
with jacket potatoes
136
New potato, basil &
pine nut salad 150
Pea, potato & rocket
soup 118
Potato & parsnip gratin
188
Potato, chickpea &
cashew curry 104
Potato gratin with pine
nut crust 188
Potato rösti with
frazzled eggs 28
Potato rösti with
poached eggs 28
Potato salad 150
Roast vegetables &
parsley pesto 160
Roasted new potatoes
with garlic &
rosemary 162
Spiced braised new
potatoes 162
pumpkin: Creamy
pumpkin, coriander and
coconut soup 122
Indian-spiced pumpkin
wedges 168
Onion, pumpkin & sage
pie 106
Pumpkin filo pie 106

Pumpkin and ricotta
cannelloni 100
Pumpkin soup with
olive salsa 116
Pumpkin with walnut
pesto 64
Vegetable tempura 164

raspberries: Honeyed
ricotta with summer
fruits 34
Raspberry sauce 204
Raspberry sorbet 216
Soufflé jam omelette
208
Very berry fruit salad
228
Relish 84
Rhubarb, pear & marzipan
crumble 232
rice 12
Asian-style risotto 96
Beetroot & goats'
cheese risotto 88
Beetroot & mascarpone
risotto with pine nuts
88
Creamy pea & mint
risotto with brie 80
Italian-style risotto 96
Mixed spice pilaf 94
Rice patties 80
Vegetable & rice soup
120
Vegetable kebabs with
pilaf 94
rocket: Bruschetta with
fig, rocket and feta 50
Pea, potato & rocket
soup 118
rocket & goats' cheese
omelette 18
rosemary: Bean, lemon &
rosemary hummus 68
Roasted new potatoes
with garlic &
rosemary 162
rosewater: Fragrant berry
and rosewater salad
228

Peach & rosewater
crush 214
**Saffron-scented**
vegetable tagine 128
salsa: Avocado salsa 42
Olive salsa 116
Pomegranate salsa 42
Tomato salsa 100
sauces: Blueberry sauce
32
Ponzu dipping sauce
164
Spiced apple sauce 32
Toffee sauce 220
sausages: Leek & thyme
sausages with relish 84
savoiardi biscuits 12
seaweed 13
seeds: Mixed seed soda
bread 180
soda bread: Mixed seed
soda bread 180
Pinhead oatmeal soda
bread 180
sorbets 216
soups 110-24
spaghetti *see* pasta
spinach: Spinach & feta
tart 176
Spinach & Gorgonzola
salad 152
Spinach & mushroom
lasagne 90
Spinach & ricotta
cannelloni 100
Spinach and goats'
cheese frittata 54
squash: Butternut squash,
tofu & pea curry 74
Roasted butternut
squash soup 116
Roasted squash & sage
pizza 192
storage 9
strawberries: Strawberry
& lavender crush 214
Summer strawberry
cream croissants 36
Very berry fruit salad
228

sugar snap peas:
Stir-fried tofu with basil
& chilli 98
swedes: Winter
vegetables & beer
broth 120
sweet potatoes: Baked
sweet potatoes 166
Crispy sweet potato
skins 166
Indian-spiced sweet
potato wedges 168
Sweet potato &
coconut soup 122
Sweet potato & fontina
panini 48
sweetcorn: Chilli &
sweetcorn cornbread
182
Sweetcorn & kaffir lime
fritters 44

**tabbouleh**, Couscous
146
tahini paste 13
tapenade: Fig, goats'
cheese & tapenade tart
174
thyme: Leek & thyme
burgers with blue
cheese 84
Leek & thyme
sausages with relish
84

Mushroom, walnut &
thyme soup 112
Tiramisù cheesecake
212
Toffee sauce 220
tofu: Butternut squash,
tofu & pea curry 74
Roasted spiced tofu 58
Stir-fried tofu with basil
& chilli 98
Tofu & vegetables in
oyster sauce 98
Tofu with chilli vinegar
dressing 58
tomatoes: All-in-one
veggie breakfast 22
Asparagus, tomato &
feta frittata 102
Aubergine & goats'
cheese gratin 186
Aubergine lasagne 186
Aubergine toasties with
pesto 86
Aubergine and tomato
curry 104
Bruschetta with
tomatoes & ricotta 50
Cheese & tomato
omelette 18
Cheese, tomato & basil
muffins 24
Cherry tomato and
cheese pizza 190
Chilli bean soup 114

Couscous tabbouleh
146
Gnocchi, plum tomato &
sage butter gratin 46
Greek country salad
with haloumi 154
Italian tricolore salad
140
Mushroom, flageolet &
tomato lasagne 90
Omelette with basil
tomatoes 92
Parmesan eggy bread
16
Provençal vegetable
stew 132
Saffron-scented
vegetable tagine 128
Spiced carrot and
tomato soup 110
Spiced couscous salad
146
Spiced tomato and
Mexican bean soup
124
Tomato & bread salad
148
Tomato & feta tart 178
Tomato salsa 100
Tomato stuffed
omelette 92
Vegetable kebabs with
pilaf 94
Truffle butter 112

**vanilla:** Apricot & vanilla
zabaglione 230
vegetable stock 13
vincotto 13
vinegar: Chilli vinegar
dressing 58

**wakame** seaweed 13
walnuts: Chocolate
walnut muffins 38
Mushroom, walnut &
thyme soup 112
Onion, walnut & blue
cheese tarts 70
Walnut pesto 64
Watercress, almond &
Stilton salad 152
Watermelon, fennel & feta
salad 144
wontons: Crispy
mushroom wontons 66
Mushroom & ginger
wonton 66
Sweet wonton
millefeuille 234

**yogurt:** Aubergine dip
with flatbreads 60
Cucumber & mint dip
60

**Zabaglione** 230

# acknowledgements

**Executive editor:** Nicola Hill
**Editor:** Ruth Wiseall
**Deputy creative director:** Karen Sawyer
**Designer:** Janis Utton
**Photographer:** Ian Wallace
**Food and props stylist:** Louise Pickford
**Production manager:** Nigel Reid

**Special photography:** © Octopus Publishing Group
Limited/Ian Wallace
**Other photography:** © Octopus Publishing Group
Limited/William Lingwood 55, 65, 79, 93, 147, 153,
195, 197, 205, 209, 215, 223, 227, 231, 233; /Lis
Parsons 37; /William Shaw 43, 175